Is the Help Helpful?

How To Create Online Help that Meets Your Users' Needs

Jean Hollis Weber

Hentzenwerke Publishing

Published by:
Hentzenwerke Publishing
980 East Circle Drive
Whitefish Bay WI 53217 USA

Hentzenwerke Publishing books are available through booksellers and directly from the publisher.
Contact Hentzenwerke Publishing at:
414.332.9876
414.332.9463 (fax)
www.hentzenwerke.com
books@hentzenwerke.com

Is the Help Helpful? How To Create Online Help that Meets Your Users' Needs
    By Jean Hollis Weber
    Technical Editor: Tamar Granor
    Copy Editor: Jeana Frazier
    Cover Art: "Rescue" by Todd Gnacinski, Milwaukee, WI

ISBN: 1-930919-60-3

Manufactured in the United States of America.

Our Contract with You, the Reader

In which we, the folks who make up Hentzenwerke Publishing, describe what you, the reader, can expect from this book and from us.

Hi there!

I've been writing professionally (in other words, eventually getting a paycheck for my scribbles) since 1974, and writing about software development since 1992. As an author, I've worked with a half-dozen different publishers and corresponded with thousands of readers over the years. As a software developer and all-around geek, I've also acquired a library of more than 100 computer and software-related books.

Thus, when I donned the publisher's cap seven years ago to produce the *1997 Developer's Guide,* I had some pretty good ideas of what I liked (and didn't like) from publishers, what readers liked and didn't like, and what I, as a reader, liked and didn't like.

Now, with our new titles for 2004, we're entering our seventh season. (For those who are keeping track, the '97 DevGuide was our first, albeit abbreviated, season, the batch of six "Essentials" for Visual FoxPro 6.0 in 1999 was our second, and, in keeping with the sports analogy, the books we published in 2000 through 2003 comprised our third and subsequent seasons.)

John Wooden, the famed UCLA basketball coach, posited that teams aren't consistent; they're always getting better—or worse. We'd like to get better…

One of my goals for this season is to build a closer relationship with you, the reader. In order for us to do this, you've got to know what you should expect from us.

- You have the right to expect that your order will be processed quickly and correctly, and that your book will be delivered to you in new condition.

- You have the right to expect that the content of your book is technically accurate and up-to-date, that the explanations are clear, and that the layout is easy to read and follow without a lot of fluff or nonsense.

- You have the right to expect access to source code, errata, FAQs, and other information that's relevant to the book via our Web site.

- You have the right to expect an electronic version of your printed book to be available via our Web site.

- You have the right to expect that, if you report errors to us, your report will be responded to promptly, and that the appropriate notice will be included in the errata and/or FAQs for the book.

Naturally, there are some limits that we bump up against. There are humans involved, and they make mistakes. A book of 500 pages contains, on average, 150,000 words and several megabytes of source code. It's not possible to edit and re-edit multiple times to catch every last misspelling and typo, nor is it possible to test the source code on every permutation of development environment and operating system—and still price the book affordably.

Once printed, bindings break, ink gets smeared, signatures get missed during binding. On the delivery side, Web sites go down, packages get lost in the mail. Nonetheless, we'll make our best effort to correct these problems—once you let us know about them.

In return, when you have a question or run into a problem, we ask that you first consult the errata and/or FAQs for your book on our Web site. If you don't find the answer there, please e-mail us at **books@hentzenwerke.com** with as much information and detail as possible, including 1) the steps to reproduce the problem, 2) what happened, and 3) what you expected to happen, together with 4) any other relevant information.

I'd like to stress that we need you to communicate questions and problems clearly. For example...

- Bad reports:

  "Your downloads don't work."

  "Your Web site is down."

  "The code in Chapter 10 caused an error."

  These types of complaints don't contain enough information for us to help you.

- Good reports:

  "I get a 404 error when I click on the **Download Source Code** link on **www.hentzenwerke.com/book/downloads.html**."

  "I performed the following steps to run the source code program DisplayTest.PRG in Chapter 10, and I received an error that said 'Variable m.liCounter not found.'"

  Now this is something we can help you with.

We'll do our best to get back to you within a couple of days, either with an answer or at least an acknowledgment that we've received your inquiry and that we're working on it.

On behalf of the authors, technical editors, copy editors, layout artists, graphical artists, indexers, and all the other folks who have worked to put this book in your hands, I'd like to thank you for purchasing this book, and I hope that it will prove to be a valuable addition to your technical library. Please let us know what you think about this book—we're looking forward to hearing from you.

As Groucho Marx once observed, "Outside of a dog, a book is a man's best friend. Inside of a dog, it's too dark to read."

Whil Hentzen
Hentzenwerke Publishing
September 2004

List of Chapters

Table of Contents

Chapter 2: Analyzing Audiences and Tasks   23

Chapter 3: Developing Specifications   35

Dedication

To Eric Lindsay, for putting up with me during the research and writing of this book, assisting with technical problems, and providing food and drink at appropriate intervals.

Acknowledgments

Numerous members of the HATT (Help Authors Tools and Techniques) and Techwr-L (Technical Writers) Internet discussion lists assisted with my research. Daniela Meleo and many other people critically commented on an earlier version of this book (titled *Editing Online Help*, self-published in 2000).

Thanks to Doug Bell for the use of his open-source program TreeLine as an example in this book, and for allowing me to put the source and compiled files on the Web site for this book.

Special thanks go to Tamar Granor for technical editing of this new book (and asking the sorts of insightful questions that required me to rewrite whole chapters), and to Jeana Frazier for her excellent copyediting. All remaining errors and omissions are my responsibility.

—Jean Hollis Weber

About the Authors

Jean Hollis Weber

Author **Jean Hollis Weber** has a Master of Science degree in botany and more than 25 years of experience as a scientific and technical editor and writer in the fields of biology, mathematics, engineering, and computing. She has worked for numerous organizations including the Commonwealth Scientific and Industrial Research Organisation (CSIRO), IBM Australia, and Lexmark International Australia, both alone on small projects and as a team member and team leader on large projects.

A technical publications consultant for the past 10 years, Jean has worked with clients, written books, taught short courses in writing and editing, and lectured to graduate and undergraduate classes in writing and editing at several Australian universities. Jean is active in the Society for Technical Communication.

A dual U.S.–Australian citizen, Jean has lived in Australia since 1974. Recently she escaped from the big cities to live in the seaside resort town of Airlie Beach, Queensland, at the gateway to the beautiful Whitsunday Islands. Jean conducts her writing and editing business over the Internet from her home and from numerous campgrounds and motel rooms on her travels around Australia.

Jean has published six previous books, including *Electronic Editing*, the *Taming Microsoft Word* series, and *Taming OpenOffice.org Writer* (now replaced by *OpenOffice.org Writer: The Free Alternative to Microsoft Word*). All of Jean's books are available through her Technical Editors' Eyrie Web site. She also publishes a free e-mailed newsletter for editors and maintains three Web sites:

- Technical Editors' Eyrie, **http://www.jeanweber.com/**

- Avalook (Australian travel for over-50's), **http://www.avalook.com.au/**

- Taming OpenOffice.org, **http://www.taming-openoffice-org.com/**

Tamar Granor

Technical Editor **Tamar E. Granor, Ph.D.,** is the owner of Tomorrow's Solutions, LLC. She has developed and enhanced numerous applications for businesses and other organizations, primarily using Visual FoxPro, including integrating it with Microsoft Office. She currently focuses on working with other developers through consulting and subcontracting. Tamar served as editor of *FoxPro Advisor* magazine from 1994 to 2000. She is currently the magazine's technical editor and coauthor of the popular Advisor Answers column.

Tamar is coauthor of *What's New in Visual FoxPro 8.0*, *Hacker's Guide to Visual FoxPro 7.0* (and its award-winning predecessor), *What's New in Visual FoxPro 7.0*, and *Microsoft Office Automation with Visual FoxPro*. She is the technical editor of *Visual FoxPro Certification Exams Study Guide*. All of these books are available from Hentzenwerke Publishing (**http://www.hentzenwerke.com**). Tamar is also coauthor of the *Hacker's Guide* *to Visual FoxPro 3.0* (Addison-Wesley); she contributed to John Hawkins' *FoxPro 2.5 Programmer's Reference* (Que).

Tamar is a Microsoft Certified Professional and a Microsoft Support Most Valuable Professional. She speaks frequently about Visual FoxPro at conferences and user groups in North America and Europe.

Tamar's years of writing, editing, presentations, and community work have given her considerable experience with Microsoft Office. She has been using OpenOffice.org for the bulk of those activities since late 2002.

Tamar earned her doctorate in Computer and Information Science at the University of Pennsylvania, where her research focused on implementation of user interfaces. Tamar lives in suburban Philadelphia with her husband and two sons.

How to Download the Files

Hentzenwerke Publishing generally provides two sets of files to accompany its books. The first is the source code or sample files referenced throughout the text. Note that some books do not have source code or sample files; in those cases, a placeholder file is provided in lieu of the source code in order to alert you of the fact. The second is the e-book version of the book, which is supplied in Adobe Acrobat (PDF) format. Here's how to get them.

Both the sample files and e-book file are available for download from the Hentzenwerke Web site. In order to obtain them, follow these instructions:

1. Point your Web browser to **http://www.hentzenwerke.com**.

2. Look for the link that says "Download."

3. A page describing the download process will appear. This page has two sections:

    - **Section 1:** If you were issued a user name/password directly from Hentzenwerke Publishing, you can enter them into this page.

    - **Section 2:** If you did not receive a user name/password from Hentzenwerke Publishing, don't worry! Just enter your e-mail alias and look for the question about your book. Note that you'll need your physical book when you answer the question.

4. A page that lists the hyperlinks for the appropriate downloads will appear.

Note that the e-book file is covered by the same copyright laws as the printed book. Reproduction and/or distribution of this file is against the law.

If you have questions or problems, the fastest way to get a response is to e-mail us at **books@hentzenwerke.com**.

Introduction

Who is this book for?

This book is intended for students, writers, and editors who are developing online help for computer software, and for their managers and clients. Readers need no prerequisites except some experience as users of online help systems.

What's in this book?

This book outlines the principles of planning, writing, editing, and testing online help, regardless of the operating system running the application, the type of help being produced, or the tools used to produce it. It supplements the many other books that teach how to use specific help-authoring tools.

In this book, you'll discover:

- The 10 most common complaints that users have with online help, the causes of the underlying problems, and ways to avoid those problems

- The 11 steps in the ideal help-development process, their benefits, and the problems that arise when a step is left out

- Techniques and examples for planning, writing, editing, reviewing, and testing online help

- Sample plan and specifications for your help project

What's not in this book?

This book does not attempt to discuss the advantages and disadvantages of the available help systems, nor cover the use of specific help-authoring tools.

New types of help keep appearing as Web-based applications and applications for other operating systems are developed. You'll need to refer to other sources of information (probably on the Web) to learn about new technologies.

Icons used in this book

Throughout this book, the following icons are used to point out special notes.

 This "note" icon calls out information of special interest, related topics, or important notes that don't fit well into the flow of the text.

 This "tip" icon marks ideas for shortcuts, alternate ways of accomplishing tasks that can make your life easier or save time, or techniques that aren't immediately obvious.

 *Paragraphs marked with this icon indicate that the referenced sample files are available for download at **http://www.hentzenwerke.com**. See the page titled "How to Download the Files" for more information.*

Chapter 1
Planning an Online Help Project

Online help is as much a part of the user interface as windows, dialog boxes, or Web pages. It must be planned and designed as part of the project, with similar consideration for users' requirements. This chapter describes an ideal planning process, the roles of the people involved in producing online help, the time required, and the work sequence for help development.

The term "online help" (sometimes called "user assistance") applies to WinHelp, Microsoft HTML Help, HTML-based help, WebHelp, JavaHelp, and other forms of online information, and includes features known as "show-me help," embedded help, and several varieties of electronic performance support systems.

Online help is information that meets these three criteria:

- Users can access it directly from the software interface (including browser-based interfaces and Web pages) by selecting an item on a Help menu, by clicking a link or button on the interface, or by pressing a key (such as F1 or Help) on the keyboard.

- It provides guidance and assistance as users complete real work tasks, not just practice tasks, as found in tutorials.

- It provides an immediate answer to a question about a specific window or dialog.

Many online help systems today also contain conceptual information and descriptions of longer, more complex tasks that require the user to access a variety of windows or dialogs—topics that traditionally have been included in printed books.

Many software products provide only an online book (in PDF, WinHelp, HTML, or other formats) and call it Help. However, online books usually are not directly linked to specific elements in the user interface, nor are they interactive. Typically, such books open at the table of contents, or at a bookmark specified by the user. Although it is possible to associate specific pages in online books with specific elements of the user interface, most applications don't provide those links. I call this information *online documentation*, to distinguish it from the type of online help discussed in this book.

Why plan an online help project?

Online help needs to work with the user interface and fit into the overall documentation set for the software product, so it should be planned and coordinated with the user interface and the other user documents, not produced in isolation or as an afterthought to the project.

Planning is particularly important when more than one person is involved in producing the online help, so that all players know their roles and how to ensure that their contributions fit together into a coordinated whole. However, even if you are a lone writer, responsible for doing everything, you need a plan; how else can you negotiate with the software developers to make sure the help you produce will fit in with the program itself?

Therefore, someone (for example, the documentation team leader, the lead writer, or the editor) needs to write an online help plan. The written plan should:

- Describe each phase of the help-development process: task analysis, design, formal reviews, editing, and testing; and the roles of the people involved at each stage of the process. Other people, such as software developers, working on the project can then use the plan to understand how their roles work together with the roles of the help writer, editor, and other people on the team.

- Be reviewed and approved by the relevant stakeholders (clients, marketing, user interface designers, and software developers) to obtain their agreement and support before major work begins on the help.

- Be updated when significant decisions are changed, or when the scope of the work significantly changes.

- Include a schedule showing links with the user interface development schedule.

- Specify all the help producers' assumptions, dependencies, and risks. What do you need from others, and when? See Table 4 in this chapter, and also Appendix A, "Sample Plans and Specifications."

Specifications should be part of the planning process for documentation as well as software. Therefore, in addition to writing the help plan, someone should write a help design specification, as described later in this chapter, in "Step 2. Develop high-level specifications" and "Step 3. Develop detailed specifications."

 A sample online help plan is provided in Appendix A and in the files available for download from the Hentzenwerke Web site.

What process is used in an ideal help project?

The ideal help project would have unlimited time and resources to produce help that meets all the needs of its target audience. It would also be well planned and the development would proceed according to the plan.

As we all know, time and resources are always limited and changes often occur at inconvenient times, so we have to make compromises. The compromises should never include skipping the planning stage of the project, yet this happens all too frequently.

Sometimes planning is not done because the people involved don't realize how much they can do before learning details about the user interface for the software product. In fact, you can do most of the planning steps without this information, as long as you know what the product is supposed to do, and who the intended audience is.

Let's look at the steps involved in the ideal help project, why each step is important, and what might happen if the step is skipped.

1. Analyze the audience, plan the project, and write the plan.

2. Develop high-level specifications.

3. Develop detailed specifications.

4. Perform a detailed task analysis.

5. Build and evaluate a prototype help system.

6. Develop an outline and map of the help project.

7. Write, index, and edit the help topics.

8. Review the help topics, index, and table of contents.

9. Test the help by itself and with the product.

10. Release the help with the product.

11. Evaluate the help and plan for improvements.

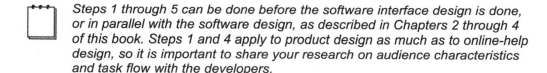 *Steps 1 through 5 can be done before the software interface design is done, or in parallel with the software design, as described in Chapters 2 through 4 of this book. Steps 1 and 4 apply to product design as much as to online-help design, so it is important to share your research on audience characteristics and task flow with the developers.*

Step 1. Analyze the audience, plan the project, and write the plan

Planning might be done by the documentation team leader, the writer, the editor, or by all of these people contributing their particular expertise. Include all planning decisions in an online help plan, and have the plan approved by the relevant people.

This step has several sub-steps, some of which should be done at the same time. If your project is an update to existing software, some of this work may have been done previously, but you should check whether any of the factors have changed for this update.

1. Describe the software product and its purpose in terms of its intended users and their tasks.

2. Analyze and profile the intended users, their knowledge and skill levels, and the tasks to be supported by the software product. See Chapter 2, "Analyzing Audiences and Tasks," for more information.

3. For products to be sold commercially, study your competitors' products, which may have influenced customer expectations.

4. Establish the main aims of the help and the purpose of each information type. See Chapter 3, "Developing Specifications," for more about information types.

5. Determine any constraints, such as:

   • Whether the software product and the help will be run on more than one operating system; if so, determine what system-specific functions cannot be used

- Any limits on help functionality imposed by the operating system, other software such as Web browsers, or accessibility requirements

- How the help will fit into the product's documentation set

- How the programmers will link the help to the product

- Whether the product and the help will be translated into other languages

- Whether the product and the help will be localized—for example, to accommodate different currencies, cultures, or taxation schemes

- How much time and money is available for the project

6. Write down other assumptions and the consequences of changes; for example:

   - The client's operating system is A.

   - Reviewers will return all review comments within X days.

   - Developers will keep to their schedule.

   - Client will not change the help specifications after they are approved.

7. Document other dependencies for the writing team and the consequences if the dependencies are not met. For example:

   - The accuracy and completeness of the product's technical specifications

   - Technical input from subject-matter experts when needed

   - Working version of product code containing realistic data available by a certain time

8. Determine other risks and define a mitigation strategy. For example, if the product is using a new platform, the method of associating the help topics may not be clearly understood. Unless the technical issues are resolved by a certain date, the completion dates for the help project are at risk.

9. Estimate the time required to plan, write, edit, review, and test the help.

10. Negotiate with developers and others to:

    - Determine realistic requirements for the help

    - Specify when the writer can get access to a working version of the software

    - Specify the type and timing of technical reviews and testing

    - Specify who will have the final authority to approve the content, and what the approval criteria will be

11. Choose professional technical communicators to write, index, and edit the help. Choose professional usability experts to advise, evaluate, and test the help as it is planned and developed.

12. Choose a help-authoring tool and any other required software, and ensure that the writer and editor know how to use it.

Benefits of this step

Good planning vastly improves your chances of completing a project on time and within budget, while producing usable, helpful, correct, and complete help. Lack of planning almost ensures that the project will run into problems.

Problems if this step is not done

The writers, developers, clients, and others may have unrealistic expectations about the complexity of the project and what is needed to do the work.

As a result, too much work must be completed in the available time, so some steps will be dropped or curtailed, or the project will run over time and over budget. For example, editing may be limited to a cursory check of spelling, grammar, and layout consistency; substantive issues may never be identified. Indexing and testing may be inadequate, contributing to usability problems. Problems often cannot be fixed, even when identified, because no time is left in which to make the changes.

Note that all these problems are greater if the help has been written by someone other than a professional technical communicator, or if it has been written by a team of communicators without overall planning and coordination.

Step 2. Develop high-level specifications

Drawing on the analysis done in Step 1, the documentation team now needs to develop high-level specifications for the help.

High-level specifications should include decisions on such issues as what information types, topic types, window types (primary, secondary, pop-up, tri-pane), and navigation aids will be used; and whether to use audio or video files. See Chapter 3, "Developing Specifications," and Appendix A, "Sample Plans and Specifications."

During this step, develop a high-level sample of the help, evaluate it, and revise it as necessary. Include screen shots of the sample in the specifications. Consider producing the specification as a help file, to demonstrate the design.

Be sure to get the client's approval of the high-level specifications, and ensure that the approved user-interface specifications refer to the help specifications.

A writer or editor should also be involved with the design of the software user interface. This person can look at such issues as: Are the instructions, icons, field names, and other words and graphics appropriate for the audience? Will the help work well with the intended user interface design?

Make sure that the help types you are planning can be linked to the user interface in a consistent way; for example, all dialogs have a Help button that is linked to a specific help topic (not always linked to the contents page), and each page in a multipage dialog has a separate link to a specific help topic.

Benefits of this step

With a specification for the online help, everyone on the project knows what's expected, and no one has to take time later figuring out what to do. The specification also leads to help that is very consistent, so the users know where to expect help, what sort of help to expect, and where they can navigate from any type of help topic.

Help can be reviewed with the users or clients to ensure that they approve the intended system, and that they know what to expect from the writing team.

Help is easier for testers to test, because they can cross check against an approved specification document.

Help is easier for technical reviewers to review, because they aren't distracted by consistency problems. Errors in help implementation are easier to detect.

The online help development process is perceived by others on the project as much more rigorous and disciplined, and the technical writers' professional standing increases accordingly.

Problems if this step is not done

The writer will have to pay more attention to design issues during the writing stage, and is more likely to forget something.

The help interface may be poorly designed or inconsistent (particularly if more than one writer is involved).

Later in the project, the editor's work will be more complex and will probably include many more consistency changes and negotiations over terminology and other issues. The chance of correcting problems later is low, due to time constraints.

Help is more difficult and time-consuming to review and test; problems may be overlooked if time is short.

Help testing scenarios cannot be adequately written if there is no help specification with which to compare the finished system.

Step 3. Develop detailed specifications

Develop detailed specifications for the online help. Include writing conventions, terminology, style sheets, and templates for topic types. See Chapter 3, "Developing Specifications," and Appendix A, "Sample Plans and Specifications." Consider producing the detailed specifications as a help file. Be sure to get the client's approval of the specifications.

This is one of the two most important planning steps, in terms of the helpfulness of the help. (The other is the task analysis.) The editor needs to develop a project-specific style guide or style sheet to record specific decisions about the format, presentation, and content of the help topics or other online documentation that will be provided for the project. The best mix of online help and other documentation is different for different applications. Work with the writer and the project leader when making the decisions.

Ensure that terms match those to be used in the user interface and the printed documentation. Create a terminology list, including terms used by your competitors but not in your product, so you can include relevant synonyms in the index of the help and the printed user documentation. The terminology list can also form the basis of a glossary and the definitions provided to the translators.

Ensure that any consistency issues between the help, the interface, and the printed documentation are resolved. Consider translation and accessibility issues.

Even when only one writer is involved, a project leader needs to consider what happens if that writer leaves the project before it is complete, and who will maintain the help in future releases.

Benefits of this step

With a plan for the detailed look and feel of the online help, everyone on the project knows what's expected, and doesn't have to take time later in the project figuring out what to do. The help should then end up very consistent, so the editor, tester, and quality-assurance people are looking mainly for deviations from the plan. The final result should be a help system that ends up being consistent, and thus not confusing to the user.

New members of the team can quickly come up to speed and fit their writing into the overall look and feel of the help.

Problems if this step is not done

Lack of a detailed design, particularly on a project involving more than one writer, often leads to inconsistency in all aspects of the help interface, including style, terminology, content, presentation, topic types, and navigation. Correcting these inconsistencies takes more time later in the project; and if the corrections are not made, users may be confused.

Step 4. Perform a detailed task analysis

The technical communication team now needs to develop a detailed task list from the intended audience's point of view. Task analysis may involve use cases, user scenarios, and other techniques. Include your task list in the help specifications. See Chapter 2, "Analyzing the Audience and Their Tasks," for some ideas.

In addition, create a list of questions that users might ask. From the task and question lists, you can begin building a list of help topics. This list will probably evolve as the project progresses, especially if the application itself is evolving.

Benefits of this step

These lists form the basis of the writer's help topics and the editorial review of the index, the table of contents, and the overall helpfulness of the help.

If task lists are compiled at this stage, the editor can check the writer's work more easily, because most questions about what should be included have been resolved.

Problems if this step is not done

Without task and question lists, the writer may forget to include some information that the users need, and the editor may fail to notice the omissions.

Step 5. Build and evaluate a prototype help system

You can build a help system prototype in two steps. For an early prototype, you don't need to know the details of the user interface, although you do need the task and question lists developed in Step 4.

You can develop many aspects of the prototype in conjunction with the specifications if you produce the specifications as a help file. You can also use placeholders such as "Procedure steps go here" and "Link to concept topic" in an early prototype.

Include at least one example of each topic type, with all relevant navigation aids, links between topic types, and other design components. Involve the software developers to ensure that your ideas fit in with their plans for coding the links between the application and the help system.

If the user interface is being prototyped at the same time, try linking the prototype help system with the product to see how it all works together. Do the topics and the planned level of topic breakdown make sense in the context of how the user interface will work?

Come back to your prototype after Step 6, build in some more detail, and evaluate it again. Ideally, you will be able to involve real users in the evaluation.

Benefits of this step
You will be able to identify ideas that don't work well in practice, and have a chance to change them before anyone starts writing. A bit of time spent here often saves more time later, when you don't have to rewrite material.

You can show the prototype to users or customers and get feedback from them about your topic types, navigation methods, linking patterns, and planned level of detail; improve your design based on their comments.

Problems if this step is not done
If you skip the prototype step, you could find (during the writing or testing stages) that some planned features of the help don't work the way you intended, and some or all of the help system might have to be redesigned or rewritten.

Step 6. Develop an outline and map of the help project
You need to develop an outline and map of your help project, showing the relationships among the various help topics and the application windows. Add this information to the help specifications. See "Outline and mapping the help project" in Chapter 4, "Prototyping the Help System," for examples.

By this stage, if not earlier, the software interface design should be available. The application programmers should have a map of the application windows, or at least a list of them, for you to use as a starting point, but their map may not have the level of detail you need. If this information is not available or is changing constantly, your challenge is greatly increased.

Help-authoring packages include various tools to assist you in developing an outline and map. Consult the documentation for the package you are using. You could also use a package such as Visio to manually prepare a map.

When making your outline and map, consider such issues as:

- One application window may be used for more than one user task.

- More than one help topic may be needed for one application window.

- One help topic may be reusable for more than one application window.

For more information, see Chapter 7, "Providing Navigation and Context," Chapter 8, "Meeting the Needs of Novices to Experts," and Chapter 9, "Linking from Application to Help."

Benefits of this step
You don't miss writing help for any windows, dialogs, and pages.

Links within the help are consistent but don't get too complex.

Testers, editors, and reviewers know which help topic is intended to be called from each application window, and don't miss any topics.

Testers, editors, and reviewers know what the internal links should be.

Problems if this step is not done

If this step is not done, writers, testers, editors, and reviewers may miss some topics, or will need to spend more time later on checking to make sure that nothing has been skipped.

Step 7. Write, index, and edit the help topics

If design planning was done, terminology agreed on, and templates written, the writer can concentrate on content in this step, and the editor can concentrate on checking the writing against the design specifications.

If working portions of the software interface are available (even if the help is not connected to it), the writer and editor can check the help against the interface. Does the help accurately describe what the users will see and what happens if they follow the written procedures?

Make sure that the product developers inform the writer and editor about software changes as soon as the decision is made, so any necessary changes can be incorporated in the help during this step. Some development processes make this information exchange difficult, as changes are frequent and often documented later, if at all. You may need to negotiate ways to ensure that writers are informed, and don't get bogged down in changing details too early in the writing process. Concentrate on the bigger picture and fill in the details as they become available and stabilized, as late in the writing cycle as possible.

If this is a revision of an existing product, the support group is an excellent source of information on where users have problems with the product. Even for a completely new product, you may be able to get good information from beta testers' feedback.

Indexes must be edited. Index entries automatically generated by help-authoring tools do not result in a good index, although they may make a good start from which to develop a useful index. For example, tools won't index terms that are used by the audience but not the software. The writer or editor must manually insert those terms into the index. All help-authoring tools provide a way for you to do this easily.

Benefits of this step

Obviously you can't skip the writing, but indexing and editing are very important, too. The benefits are more to the user and to help-desk and other support personnel, than to the development and testing team.

Problems if this step is not done

Inconsistencies, grammatical errors, inadequate indexes, and unhelpful topics are not detected, although they may be detected during the review step.

If problems are not detected, they can lead to poor user perceptions and an increase in support calls.

If software changes are not communicated to the writer, errors may be detected in the next (review) step, leading to extra work, or they may slip through undetected.

Users may see the help as unhelpful or unprofessional.

Step 8. Review the help topics

The software developers or other subject-matter experts typically do this step. Usability experts should also be involved. If possible, include your clients and some users and their managers. See "Methods for editing and reviewing" later in this chapter for some suggestions.

Writers then make necessary changes to the help. The writing team should use a change-control procedure to track changes arising from changes to the application as well as those arising from reviewers' comments. Help-development packages include tools for tracking who is writing, editing, or reviewing individual topics and when changes occur.

Developers and others should sign off on the content of the help at the end of this step.

Benefits of this step

Help that has been technically reviewed is more likely to be accurate, especially if changes were made to the design of the application after the design documents were prepared.

Help that has been reviewed by usability experts is more likely to be helpful to the users.

Problems if this step is not done

If previous planning steps have been done well, major problems should not persist until this stage. However, technical reviews may be limited to the technical accuracy of the help file's contents, with no one assigned to review helpfulness.

Step 9. Test the help

Test the help by itself and with the software. Include the table of contents and the index in the testing. Revise the help as needed. See Chapter 11, "Usability Testing on a Budget." Ensure that details of the expected help-testing process have been included in the approved help plan, because testers often do not realize what is involved in thorough testing of online help (see "What types of testing are required?" later in this chapter). Ensure that the test team is formally committed to test the help in the way specified in the plan. Plan ways to involve the product's beta testers in testing the help.

Benefits of this step

Help that has been tested is more likely to work as intended, with no broken links or missing topics (which may be in the help file but not be connected to the appropriate parts of the software or other help topics) and no topics linked incorrectly to the application.

Problems if this step is not done

Untested help may have broken links, missing topics, or incorrectly connected topics.

Step 10. Release the help with the product

Beta or test versions of software may be released without a help system, or with an early draft of the help system, but a rollout of finished software includes a fully written, indexed, edited, and tested help system.

Benefits of this step

Users can access the help system and find what they want and need. Support personnel should notice a decline in requests for assistance.

Problems if this step is not done

If major errors have persisted until the release of the system, or the wrong copy of the help is released with the software, the biggest problems are embarrassment to the help-development team, annoyance to the users, loss of confidence in the help and the product, and increased calls to the help desk. In commercial products, such errors could lead to loss of sales.

Step 11. Evaluate the help and plan for improvements

After the product is shipped, involve users in evaluating the help. For example, you could include an e-mail link in each topic, to encourage users to provide feedback. Open-source products tend to have some defect-tracking mechanism that lets users report defects in the help as well as in the product. Plan improvements for the next release. This step is outside the scope of this book.

Benefits of this step

You'll do it even better next time, and everyone will benefit.

Problems if this step is not done

If the team doesn't learn from its mistakes, it's doomed to repeat them.

What are the roles in an online help project?

Producing an online help project requires people to fill many roles. Some of the roles that might be required include:

- Project manager/planner/producer
- Writer
- Editor
- Graphic artist or illustrator
- Instructional designer
- Programmer
- Multimedia producer
- Indexer
- Localization and translation coordinator
- Usability tester
- Quality assurance (QA) person

 In some projects, one person may fill most or all of the roles; other projects may involve teams of several people.

Everyone on the team should be involved in the planning stages so they can contribute their expertise to the plan and ensure that the plan includes a detailed description of their roles, responsibilities, and authority; and the cost, timing, dependencies, and assumptions for all required tasks.

Project manager/planner/producer's role

JoAnn Hackos (*Managing Your Documentation Projects*, 1994) sums up the project manager's role this way: "A project manager is like the conductor of an orchestra ... The conductor assumes that all the musicians are proficient in playing their individual instruments and know their individual parts, but need leadership to work together most effectively ... the conductor envisions how all the individual sounds must fit together to result in a pleasing whole that delights the audience."

Project managers should:

- Communicate with team members and other managers
- Oversee, coordinate, and if necessary write the project plan
- Acquire and allocate resources
- Track progress against the plan
- Negotiate and make decisions as necessary to manage changes in the plan, or to resolve conflicts

Writer's role

The writer's role can be quite complex. Depending on the size of the team, writers may be responsible for editing, graphic design, layout, programming, and testing, in addition to research and actual writing. Writers should:

- If necessary, write or coordinate the help project plan
- Research the required information; if necessary, consult with software developers and other subject-matter experts
- Write the required topics, following the specifications, style guide, and other project and company standards
- Determine the suitability of material for the target audience; for example, the level of detail, technical assumptions, and tone
- Coordinate and communicate with other team members to produce and link illustrations, audio, video, and other content as needed
- Organize reviews, editing, and testing of written materials
- Track time against the schedule and alert manager to any problems
- Review, edit, and rewrite all copy as necessary, in cooperation with the editor, reviewers, and other writers

Editor's role

The editor's role should be far more than simply checking the help for grammar and spelling errors after the writing is done. Copy editing is important, but developmental, structural, technical, and usability editing are also vital to the success of the project. Editors should:

- Produce an editing plan as part of the overall project plan
- Set and enforce company standards for online and print documents and, in consultation with writers, for a particular project; or interpret and adapt company standards to the needs of a particular project

- Review and enforce company standards for user interface design—particularly those standards relating to word usage and consistency in the interface
- Coordinate the production of the online help and other user documents on one product, especially when these are written by different people
- Determine the suitability of material for the target audience; for example, the level of detail, technical assumptions, and tone
- Assist writers in the development of material, particularly its logical order and structure
- Advise writers on the appropriate use of graphics, wording of headings, figure and table captions, topic types, and index and glossary entries
- Review, test, edit, and rewrite all copy as necessary, in cooperation with writers

Graphic artist's or illustrator's role

Although many writers create their own graphics (often screen captures, flow charts, and other relatively simple illustrations), graphic artists may be involved. If animations or other complex graphics are required, a graphic artist can often produce better material in less time. Graphic artists should:

- Produce a graphics-design plan as part of the overall project plan
- Suggest additional or alternative ways to use graphics to present information
- Choose or design icons and other elements of the help, to be consistent with other publications for the product
- Crop, edit, annotate, and otherwise clean up screen captures
- Provide advice to writers on color choices, resolution, file types, file size, and other technical matters related to screen captures and other illustrations
- Create graphics to illustrate processes or concepts
- Create animations and assist in the development of online tutorials
- Design packaging and covers, as needed

Instructional designer's role

Online help often fills a training need, either through procedural topics or through explicit tutorials, embedded help, or a performance-support system. Instructional designers are experienced at breaking complex tasks into chunks and providing each chunk at an appropriate level of explanation for the audience. Instructional designers should:

- Produce an online training plan as part of the overall project plan
- Suggest ways to improve the presentation of instructional information, including procedures as well as tutorials, show-me topics, and other performance-support materials
- Assist writers in breaking complex tasks into chunks suitable for different audiences, and advise on ways to link this material

Programmer's role

Some online help projects require programming input to make them work. For example, Web pages might be dynamic (assembled from chunks of content in a database) rather than static. Writers may have the expertise to do the programming themselves, but if not (or if the job is too big for the writer to do everything), a programmer might be involved. Programmers should:

- Produce an online help programming plan as part of the overall project plan
- Set up required programming such as JavaScript modules or links to databases of content
- Assist writers to integrate programming into the help, or do the integration
- Test the help to ensure that the programming works as intended

Multimedia producer's role

If you plan to include audio, video, animations, or interactivity in your help system, a multimedia expert can help—indeed, such an expert may be essential. Multimedia producers should:

- Produce a multimedia plan as part of the overall project plan
- Advise on suitable media, considering the audience, the product, and the time and money available to do the work
- Produce or oversee production of materials
- Work closely with writer and programmer to incorporate multimedia material into the help

Indexer's role

Indexing is a specialized skill. Unfortunately, most project leaders expect writers to do their own indexing, a process that often means the index may be good for some parts of the audience, but useless for others. When more than one writer is working on one project, the resulting index is likely to be inconsistent in content, organization, and presentation. A good editor can help clean up the index and improve its consistency and usability, but an experienced indexer can make everyone's job easier and create a much better result. Indexers should:

- Produce an indexing plan as part of the overall project plan
- Become familiar with the product and its audience
- Either create the index, or work with the writer to produce the index—perhaps the writer creates index entries and the indexer amends or adds to them as necessary

Localization and translation coordinator's role

Will your product and its documentation be localized or translated? If so, will the work be done in-house or contracted to a specialist localization or translation company? The need to localize can have a major impact on timing for help. (Typically, help and the user interface get frozen well before the internals of the product.)

Localization and translation coordinators should:

- Produce a localization and translation plan as part of the overall project plan
- Work with writer, illustrator, and others to ensure that materials are produced in ways that make localization or translation easier and faster
- Coordinate the work of localizing or translating the content
- Organize testing of the resulting materials

Usability tester's role

Usability testing is essential for producing good user documentation, because it determines whether the material is suitable for the audience. Usability testers should:

- Produce a usability testing plan as part of the overall project plan, which clearly states exactly what the usability test will cover
- Conduct usability testing of the help, preferably starting with an early prototype so that changes can be made as early as possible in the writing cycle
- Make recommendations on ways to solve any problems identified during usability testing
- Follow up by usability testing the revised materials

Quality assurance (QA) person's role

Quality assurance is an area where responsibilities vary greatly from one company to another. Depending on how your company defines "quality," and whether the definition covers online help in addition to the software itself, QA may include usability testing as well as other activities. Quality assurance people should:

- Produce a quality-assurance plan as part of the overall project plan, which clearly states exactly what type of testing or other work the QA person will do
- Do whatever activities are identified for this role
- Make recommendations on ways to solve any problems identified during QA activities
- Follow up by reviewing the revised materials

How much time is required for producing online help?

Technical communicators have developed many schemes for estimating the time required to produce online help and other forms of documentation. In this section I summarize some "rules of thumb" for estimating, which work well as a starting point for a group that's never worked together before. If your department has data on past performance, use that data instead of these generic figures.

Overall time required

JoAnn Hackos (*Managing Your Documentation Projects*, 1994, p. 170) suggests an average total of 4 hours per topic, to cover all activities: planning, researching, writing, editing, indexing, reviewing, and usability testing.

This time estimate assumes that some topics will be quite short, while others will be longer and more complex. The average length is assumed to be between half and one printed page in a manual (for years the industry worked on an average of "a page a day," where a day is assumed to be 8 hours). If your project consists mainly of long topics, you may need to increase the average time estimated.

Time required for different activities

How is the total time divided among the activities? You can find a lot of numbers in the technical communication literature, but they are all much the same. Your situation may vary, so use these figures only as a starting point for developing your own estimates, and refine them as you gain experience with your clients and projects.

For example, Sun Technical Publications' style guide (*Read Me First!*, 2003, p. 283) suggests the times shown in **Table 1**. **Table 2** gives an overall set of metrics that I use, and **Table 3** breaks down editing time estimates by task, based on my personal experience.

Table 1. Productivity formulas (from Sun, 2003).

Activity	Formula for calculating hours
Writing new text	3-5 hours per page
Revising existing text	1-3 hours per page
Editing	6-8 pages per hour
Indexing	5 pages per hour
Production preparation	5 percent of all other activities
Project management	10-15 percent of all other activities

Table 2. Time required for different activities (my estimates).

Activity	Percent of total time
Planning and research	10-15
Project management	10
Writing, illustrating, other production tasks	60-65
Editing	10
Testing	5

Table 3. Time required for editing online help (my estimates).

Activity	Time required
Develop design specifications, style guide, templates	40-80 hours (note 1)
Edit substantively, including some rewriting	2-4 topics per hour
Edit table of contents	2 hours (note 2)
Copy edit	6-12 topics per hour
Light copy edit (skim help, correcting obvious errors in spelling, grammar, punctuation, consistency, and completeness)	12-30 topics per hour
Check links against specifications (Do they go to the right place? Are they useful links?)	50-70 links per hour (note 3)
Edit index (500 entries)	1 hour quick check 4+ hours detailed check, no fixes 5-20+ hours to fix problems
Quality or production edit	60-100 topics or more per hour (note 4)

Notes:
1. The time required depends on whether you're adapting or updating an existing specification and style guide, or starting from scratch; whether you need a lot of negotiation with other stakeholders (and revision of the specifications); and to some extent whether the project uses one author or several. You'll need to allow time to revise these materials after the first edit of sample material or the first review of a prototype design.
2. You may need more time to edit a very large project or a badly organized table of contents, especially if more than one writer is involved, or if the editor needs to make detailed suggestions on how to reorganize the contents.
3. Depending on the complexity of the linking system used in your project, the time required could be considerably longer than suggested here.
4. Depending on the complexity of the project and the number of tables and graphics, the time required could be considerably longer than suggested here.

Number of help topics required

Time estimates depend on the number of pages (or topics) of material that must be written, edited, reviewed, and tested. Here are some ways to estimate the number of topics. Plan to revise these estimates as the project develops.

- From functional specifications for the software, you can get an idea of the number of screens/pages/dialogs in the product and the number of fields and controls on typical screens. From these figures (no matter how preliminary), you can estimate the number of field-level and dialog-level help topics required.

- From your audience and task analysis, you can estimate the number of conceptual, task, procedural, tutorial, or other topics that may be required.

Who does what, when?

You need to work with the software developers, testers, and other players to make sure everyone understands the types of edits, reviews, and testing required for online help, and who is doing which type. Make these decisions during Step 1 of planning your help project, and include the decisions and agreements in your help plan. See "How many reviews are needed, and when?" later in this chapter for guidelines on the timing of edits and reviews.

Organizing the flow of writing, editing, reviewing, and testing

The best way to organize the division and flow of writing, editing, and reviewing depends on the individuals involved, the project, and the organization. Some questions to consider:

- How many people are involved in the project?

- What are their skill levels (as writers or editors, and as users of the tools)?

- Does everyone have access to the hardware and software required?

- What are the time constraints?

- How much other work does each person have to do?

- At what stage is a document reviewed by a subject-matter expert or other person who looks at the accuracy of the content?

- How well do team members get along with each other? Do they respect and value each other's work (both methods and results)?

- What methods will be used for reviewing and editing? (See "Methods for editing and reviewing" later in this chapter.)

 Be sure to get agreement on how the help will be reviewed, edited, and tested, and record the agreement in the help plan.

Stages of help and software development

The development stages for online help and other documentation run in parallel with the development stages of the software itself. **Table 4** compares the steps outlined in this chapter with the stages of software development, and lists critical dependencies.

How many reviews are needed, and when?

Online help should be reviewed for technical accuracy by software developers and subject-matter experts, and edited (both substantively and copyedited) just as printed documentation is reviewed and edited.

Online help should be edited and reviewed online, either in addition to a hard-copy review or in place of a hard-copy review. A major reason for this requirement is that pop-up and other linked material often does not make sense on hard copy and it is not always easy or even possible for reviewers to determine which popup is used in a particular situation. See "Methods for editing and reviewing" later in this chapter.

Table 4. *Stages of software development and help development.*

Do this help-development step	During this software-development stage	Critical dependencies for each help-development step
1. Audience analysis, high-level task analysis, help plan 2. High-level help specs	Feasibility study Requirements definition Functional specifications High-level design specs	Requirements, audience, high-level task list
3. Detailed help specs	Detailed design specs	Functional specs, high-level design specs
4. Detailed task analysis 5a. High-level prototype	Software prototype	Functional specs, high-level design specs, detailed task list
5b. Detailed prototype 6. Outline and map 7. Write, index, edit	Coding, unit testing	Detailed software design specs
8. Technical reviews	Integration testing	Reviewers available
9. Test the help	System testing Usability testing	Working software, help integrated with software
10. Release help	Product release	Help integrated with software
11. Evaluate	Evaluate	Feedback from users

For a new product or a major revision of an existing product, I suggest you perform the reviews and edits listed in **Table 5**.

Table 5. *Number and timing of reviews.*

Review	Who	When
High-level specifications	Client, product developers, editor	Planning and product high-level design
Detailed specifications	Client, product developers	Planning and product detailed design
First prototype	Client, product developers, editor	Product prototype
Completed topic outline or map	Client, editor	Product development
Copyediting	Editor	Just before content review but after initial indexing
Content, accuracy, completeness, helpfulness	Product developers or subject-matter experts	System test
Second copyedit	Editor	Just before second-draft review
Second-draft review (material 100 percent complete)	Product developers or subject-matter experts	User acceptance testing, or its equivalent
Testing	Testers, writers, or editor	User acceptance testing

What types of testing are required?

Online help is typically tested to see if the links work, but other forms of testing are needed.

Test of internal links, also called reliability testing

The documentation team is usually responsible for testing all internal links within the online help. Do they work? Do they link to the correct topics?

Test of external links

The test team is usually responsible for testing all external links—that is, the links between the application software and the help file. To assist the testers, you need to provide a map or table listing what help topic should be linked with each application window. Make sure the test team understands the necessity to test the accuracy of the links, or if you can't get agreement for the testers to do that, plan for writers or editors to test those links. Ask the developers to produce an error message that gives the missing help topic ID when a help file is not found.

Is the help helpful?

As with printed documentation, technically correct online help is not necessarily helpful to the user. A usability expert, business analyst, or other suitably qualified person should review the help from the user's perspective. Does it answer questions that a user is likely to ask in a given situation? Can the user find required information using the index or navigation tools provided? Are the cross-references and pop-ups useful or confusing? In general, is the help helpful? See Chapters 5 through 9 for more details.

In addition to other editing tasks, the technical editor for the project may also be responsible for reviewing the help for helpfulness.

Because many developers involve potential clients or users in the cycle, the writing team should do everything possible to include a sample of users in the reviews, too. Real users are the best people to judge the help.

Methods for editing and reviewing

Reviewers and editors can record their comments using various methods. Each method has advantages and disadvantages, some of which depend on the available technology, the stage of development of the help system and/or the software it documents, the location of the writers, the skill levels of the writer and editor (both using the tool and in writing or editing), the working environment and its pecking order, whether a writer is still on the project, and the requirements of auditors.

Online help should always be reviewed, edited, and tested using a working copy of the help file using the same software as users (operating system, help viewer, Web browser). In addition, editors and reviewers might use paper copies or RTF or PDF files to check sample topics for writing style or technical accuracy of the information.

 Reviewers and editors may use different methods at different stages of help development. At some stage, help must be reviewed, edited, and tested using a working copy of the help file.

This section describes some common methods for reviewing and editing online help. **Table 6** summarizes the advantages and disadvantages of various methods.

Table 6. Advantages and disadvantages of common methods of reviewing and editing online help.

Reviewing/editing method	Is markup easily related to text and topic?	Is markup easy to do?	Does reviewer need copy of help authoring tool?	Is double handling required?
Annotations in compiled help	Maybe	No	Maybe	Yes
Separate comments file	No	No	No	Yes
Printouts annotated by hand	Yes	Yes	No	Yes
RTF or other editable files	Yes	Yes	No, but may need other software	Maybe
PDF files	Maybe	No	No, but may need Adobe Acrobat	Yes
Changes typed directly into help source file	Yes	Yes	Yes	No

Compiled help with annotations
Some software allows reviewers to make comments or annotations to a copy of the compiled help and send the comments to the writer, who makes changes to the help file itself.

Compiled help with separate comments file
Reviewers use compiled help, but type their comments into a separate file or e-mail message, and then send the file to the writer.

Compiled help printed and annotated by hand
Reviewers use compiled help, print the topics, write on the paper, and give the pages to the writer. A variation is for reviewers to receive a printed copy of the help file (produced in various ways, including output as a manual with pop-ups as footnotes, available in major help authoring tools).

RTF, Microsoft Word, or other editable files
Writer distributes the help as RTF or Microsoft Word files. Reviewers insert changes and comments into the file, using Word's revision feature, and writer transfers the comments to the working help file. Compiled help may be distributed with the editable files.

PDF files
Writer saves the help in PDF format. Reviewers annotate the PDF file (requires Adobe Acrobat, not just Adobe Reader) or print the PDF file and write on the paper. Compiled help may be distributed with the PDF files.

Changes typed directly into help source file

Editor types changes directly into the help source file. This method is not common, but it might be used when a project involves many writers, each responsible for only a few topics, and the final help system is produced by the editor or the leader of the writing team.

Choosing help-development tools

Before choosing help-development tools, decide what type of help you need for your project, and whether you intend to use the same material for both printed and online formats. Then choose tools to help you create that type of help. For more information, see Chapter 3, "Developing Specifications," and Appendix B, "Help Types and Tools."

Conclusion

Planning includes analyzing the audience, developing specifications for the help, defining the roles and the sequence of work to be done by the contributors, estimating the time required to complete the project, choosing the methods of reviewing and editing the help, and choosing help-development tools.

Updates and corrections to this chapter can be found on Hentzenwerke's Web site, **www.hentzenwerke.com**. Click "Catalog" and navigate to the page for this book.

Chapter 2
Analyzing Audiences and Tasks

Online help must be designed to meet its users' needs, which may be quite different from the needs of the software developers. Most users want task-oriented help; some users may also want function-oriented help. Developers typically want function-oriented help. This chapter describes techniques for analyzing audiences and their tasks, including developing user profiles and scenarios.

Most software applications have several audiences, each with different tasks and skill levels.

The actual or potential user base for a product, or class of products, may be wider than you think; therefore, the range of users' tasks, expectations, knowledge, and skill levels may be wider than you think. To make informed decisions about the content and presentation of online help, you need to understand as much as possible about the users and their tasks.

This chapter mentions several techniques for audience and task analysis, but it does not attempt to cover them in depth. An in-depth discussion could easily take a whole book. To learn more about the techniques mentioned here, see Appendix C, "For More Information."

Audience and task analysis is essentially the same for printed manuals, online help, and the software product itself.

Who are the audiences?

You can get information about a product's audiences from several sources. The best source is the users themselves, through surveys, focus groups, site visits, or user support groups. Help authors often don't get a chance to talk with real users, so you may have to get all your information from the product manager and your company's marketing, training, and support and service departments. (You might get different answers from different departments.) To whom is the product marketed? What do they see as the characteristics of the target market? These questions apply as much to in-house products and open-source products as they do to commercial products. Lastly, do you see other potential markets, or audience characteristics that haven't been mentioned by the people you ask?

Some audience characteristics to consider:

- Demographics: age, gender, education level, socioeconomic level, cultural background, disabilities

- Previous experience with computers and with this type of product

- Reason for using product: business or job, personal work, pleasure

- Role: What will the audience members be doing with the product, or how will it fit into their work?

- Attitudes toward the product: for example, frightened or eager, willing or hesitant

- Learning style: for example, active (doing something immediately) or reflective (thinking about it first), and preferring printed words, pictures, or spoken words

- Conditions of use: for example, office environment, factory or workshop environment, outdoors, traveling (on plane or in car)

- Type of computer: for example, desktop, laptop, palmtop; and its processing speed, memory, and operating system (Windows, Macintosh, Linux, other)

- Type of network, if any

- Other available hardware and software

- Type of Internet connection (broadband or dial-up) and reliability of connection, if relevant

In some cases, the range of some characteristics may be relatively narrow ("young teenage girls from affluent families"); in other cases, the range may be quite wide ("users of word processors" can be almost anyone).

Some traps to avoid include stereotyping the audience ("women over 60 are novice computer users with secondhand computers") or assuming that the characteristics of a past audience will be unchanged in the future ("Linux users are willing and able to figure out everything for themselves"). In the latter case, consider that as more companies and individuals move from Windows to Linux systems, the user base will include many more users with very different expectations and knowledge levels.

Avoid stereotyping audiences or assuming that audiences for a new or revised product will be the same as the audiences for existing or previous products.

JoAnn Hackos (*Managing Your Documentation Projects*, 1994, pages 129-132) gives a good example of a detailed report on audience analysis and the resulting profiles. Taking this a step further, Hackos and Dawn Stevens (*Standards for Online Communication*, 1997, pages 31-46) describe the characteristics of users in five "stages of use" (levels of knowledge and experience): Novice, Advanced Beginner, Competent Performer, Proficient Performer, and Expert Performer. These stages of use are discussed in more detail in Chapter 8, "Meeting the Needs of Novices to Experts."

Some of the planning examples in this chapter are based on real software; other examples are based on hypothetical software. The real software, TreeLine, is open source. It is available for download from the Hentzenwerke Web site.

Example 1. Audience analysis for TreeLine

This example is taken from TreeLine, an information storage program. The program's author, Doug Bell, says, "Some would call TreeLine an Outliner, others would call it a PIM [Personal Information Manager]... [It] stores almost any kind of information. A tree structure makes it easy to keep things organized... The output ... can be shown on the screen, printed, or exported to HTML."

Bell hasn't said anything about the audiences for this product, so let's take a few guesses.

- Users could be any age and from any background, but they probably have had some experience with PIMs or at least are familiar with the concept, even if they've never got around to using one themselves.

- They may have used a PIM at school or work, but not on their personal computers.

- If Linux users, they are more comfortable with a graphical user interface (GUI), not a command-line interface. (Windows users are GUI users by definition.)

- They're probably using TreeLine because they want to, rather than being told by their boss that they have to.

- They're probably using the program on a desktop or laptop computer in a home environment, rather than walking around a factory floor or other "field" situation, where a handheld or palmtop machine (which runs its own PIM software) would be more suitable.

- They might have older hardware or software and want a program that doesn't use a lot of memory or processing power.

- They might have a dial-up connection to the Internet, but no connection is required except for downloading the program.

Example 2. Audience analysis for a multi-user database program

Many business databases are very large, with legal requirements for data security and privacy. Such programs are typically used by large numbers of staff members who enter and edit data, extract reports, and perform other functions. In some cases, customers can view, edit, and print their own data as well as look up information in the database. Think of such well-known Web-based interfaces as Amazon, eBay, and PayPal; an airline booking system; or your own bank.

A large multi-user database has at least two, and probably three, main audiences: database administrators, company staff members (help desk, accounting, marketing, and other personnel), and customers. The characteristics of these three groups vary considerably; certainly their tasks, their level of access to the database, and what they need to know about its internal workings are quite different.

Working with user profiles and personas

User profiles and personas are additional tools in your audience analysis. Profiles and personas are designed to help programmers and writers focus their attention on the audiences' goals and tasks, rather than on the program's features and functions. Profiles and personas are also valuable to software testers, quality-assurance personnel, trainers, and others.

Profiles of typical users are often created by the marketing department, or by business analysts and others on the software development team, ideally with input from writers, trainers, and others who may have experience with real users.

If you're working on a project that does not already have user profiles, you may want to create your own. (If you do, the programmers, marketing people, trainers, and others may want to use them, too, so be sure to tell those people what you've done and ask for their suggestions.)

Personas and user profiles benefit many people on a project, not just the help team, so be sure to share them; you may not need to create your own.

The difference between profiles and personas may be just a matter of terminology, but in some cases, a "profile" is a list of characteristics of a typical user in a specific user category, and a "persona" is a fictional person who has those characteristics.

To create personas, start with your audience analysis and describe one or more typical users in more detail. Tell a story about each of them, as if you were writing about a real person. Be specific about details such as their job titles, age, gender, disabilities, where they live, attitudes (toward computers in general and your software in particular), learning style, knowledge and experience, and anything else that's relevant to the story you are developing. Sometimes a photograph helps you focus on a specific person.

If you have several distinct categories of users, be sure to create at least one persona for each category.

The number of personas you need to develop depends on how many categories of people are likely to use your product and the online help. These categories should emerge from your audience analysis.

Choose personas that are relevant to your situation, but don't develop any more than the minimum necessary to include the major characteristics that are important to consider when writing help. As with the initial audience analysis, avoid stereotyping users when developing personas; you want the personas to seem like real people, but you don't want to accidentally ignore some important characteristics simply because they don't fit your mental image of the characters you've chosen.

Don't create too many personas, but don't ignore any important audience characteristics that don't fit one or two personas.

The first time you develop personas, you might find you need to add details to them, or even add or delete a persona, as the project develops. Look upon this as a learning experience; as you get more practice, you're more likely to get it right the first time.

Example 3. Personas for TreeLine

Here are two personas for the TreeLine program.

Tim A. is a 57-year-old freelance journalist. He has stacks of handwritten notes on ideas for articles and research supporting those ideas: Web sites, e-mail and newsgroup postings, pages in books, and contact names and phone numbers. He also has photocopies and printouts of material, as well as files saved on his computer. He tries to keep the paper organized in manila folders and ring binders, but some things are relevant to more than one topic, so cross-referencing them is a problem, and keeping track of the hard copies and the computer files gets confusing. Tim hates wasting time chasing down all the information he wants for an article, when he needs it; he knows he's got it there somewhere, but it's hard to find.

Tim has a broadband Internet connection and an older desktop computer with somewhat out-of-date software (Microsoft Windows 98 and Office 97) that serves his needs quite well. He knows how to use e-mail, a browser, a word processor, and other tools of his trade, but he doesn't know much about their technical aspects and is completely uninterested in learning. If he has a problem with the hardware or software, he calls his son or a friend for help. Tim doesn't want to upgrade his software or install new programs, because he doesn't want to spend time learning how to use them. On the other hand, he wants to organize his notes better, so he's willing to try something new, as long as it's easy to use and the help or manual tells him exactly what to do; he doesn't want to have to figure it out for himself.

Emma B. is a 22-year-old university student. Her parents can't help her financially, so she's on a tight budget. Most of her research is done on the university's machines, but she has a secondhand laptop running Linux and other open-source software, for personal use and for essay writing at home. Her needs for organizing a lot of information are similar to Tim's, but her attitude toward software is very different. Emma hates the "hand-holding" type of online help that tells her the steps to follow (which she usually considers obvious) but doesn't answer her real questions. She's used to working with databases, she likes to know what's going on behind the scenes with the software she uses, and she likes to be able to customize her experience as much as possible.

What are the audiences' tasks?

During or after your audience analysis, you need to develop a high-level task list from the intended audience's point of view. Later, in the prototyping stage, you will need a detailed task list. As with audience analysis, much of this work may have already been done by the software developers or others. Try to be part of the team that does task analysis; if necessary, do it yourself.

Task analysis starts with a list of what the audience will do with the software, why they will do it, when, and how. Techniques include surveys, interviews, and direct observation of users doing real work. In Example 3, you observed Tim A's efforts to keep his research notes in some semblance of order, so although at this point you don't know just how he will use TreeLine, you have a good idea of why, when, and how he will use it. That's a good start; from there you can start developing a task list.

 Task analysis starts with a list of what the audience will do with the software, why they will do it, when, and how. Organize the tasks into groups, identify subtasks, and determine which tasks are required, optional, or conditional.

Once you have a task list, you can start analyzing and organizing the tasks into groups, identifying subtasks and determining which tasks and subtasks are required, optional, or conditional.

In addition, ask questions such as: "What skill level is needed by the person performing the task? What prior knowledge is needed to perform the task well? How often is the task performed? How difficult will the task be for the 'average' audience member? How critical is the task? What are the consequences of doing it wrong? Is it possible to recover?" This list of questions is taken from JoAnn Hackos' *Managing your Documentation Projects*, 1994, which includes good examples of a a high-level task description, a user/task matrix (see Example 5 later in this chapter), and a detailed task analysis.

For a relatively small, simple program like TreeLine, you won't need to go into that level of detail; but for a large, complex program, a highly detailed task analysis is necessary.

Beware of false or artificial tasks, which are software features or functions rather than real user tasks. For example, "using the customer inventory window" is an artificial task; "adding a customer order," "searching for a customer," and "checking a customer's order" are real tasks.

After you've compiled a list or matrix of audience characteristics and tasks, you need to analyze that information by using techniques such as task maps, flow diagrams, use cases, and user scenarios. Task maps and flow diagrams help you work out relationships among tasks; use cases and user scenarios describe the sequence of steps or subtasks within tasks.

You don't need to use all the techniques mentioned here. Pick the techniques that are most appropriate for your product, its audiences, and their tasks.

Example 4. User task analysis for TreeLine

Let's guess what typical users' tasks are. Here's a clue from the program's author: "Do you have lots of sticky notes lying around with various useful information jotted down? Or many lists of books, movies, website logins, personal contacts, or things to do? Can you find them when you need them? Well, I often couldn't. [TreeLine]'s my answer."

More information about the program's features and how to use it is given in the readme file for the TreeLine program, which is included in the supplementary material for this book. Working from the readme file, I've compiled this list of user tasks (after installation):

- Enter information by typing
- Enter information by importing from another source
- Organize information into "nodes"
- Move information from one node to another
- Copy information from one node to another
- Edit information or nodes
- Delete information or nodes
- Format information (for example, numbers, date, time, text, true/false)
- Find information in the database by using various selection criteria or filters
- Sort retrieved information

- Print retrieved information
- Export retrieved information in various forms, including text and HTML

Example 5. User/task matrix for a multi-user database program

The audience analysis in Example 2 showed that a large multi-user database program would have at least three distinct user groups: database administrators, company staff members, and customers. Each user group would have different tasks, as shown in **Figure 1**. A real user/task matrix would have more detailed tasks, not the very high-level ones shown here.

User tasks	User group		
	Database admins	**Company staff**	**Customers**
Set up and maintain database	X		
Produce company reports		X	
View, edit, and print personal data		X	X

Figure 1. Example of a high-level user/task matrix (much simplified).

Example 6. Task map for TreeLine

A task map lists the subtasks that relate to an overall task, and points to the topics that provide instructions for completing those tasks. It also may cross-reference related tasks. Each task map should include a brief description and list any prerequisite tasks and follow-up tasks.

Figure 2 shows part of a task map for the TreeLine program.

Task: Organize information		
Description	Set up tree structure suitable for organizing the information	
Prerequisites	None	
Subtasks		
Set up nodes	Required	(cross-reference to subtask map)
Move a node	Optional, conditional (node must exist)	(cross-reference to subtask map)
Copy a node	Optional, conditional (node must exist)	(cross-reference to subtask map)
Delete a node	Optional, conditional (node must exist)	(cross-reference to subtask map)
Follow-up tasks	None	
Related tasks	Input information	(cross-reference to subtask map)
	Output information	(cross-reference to subtask map)
	Organize nodes into categories	(cross-reference to subtask map)
Related concepts	Relationships of categories, nodes (parent/child), references	

Figure 2. Part of a task map for the TreeLine program.

In many cases, task maps are used only as aids to programmers, writers, testers, and others on the development team. In some cases, task maps might be included in the help file or user manual, as an aid to users.

Come back to the task map as you develop your prototype (see Chapter 4, "Prototyping the Help System") and cross-reference the task map to a task-topic map (see Figure 4).

Flow diagram

If a task is complex, you can use a flow diagram to guide you through the task. Flow diagrams may be used only as aids to programmers, writers, testers, and others on the development team, or they may be included in the help file or user manual.

When used as a writing aid, flow diagrams can be quickly and easily constructed from sticky notes (the physical, not electronic, variety) placed on a large piece of paper and connected by bits of string or pencil lines. This technique allows for rapid rearrangement of the diagram as you analyze the tasks and subtasks; later you can re-create the diagram in a flowcharting program to include it in the help plan or in the help itself.

When prototyping the help system, you'll relate the task flow diagram to the actual dialogs, windows, and pages of the software. Sometimes this exercise reveals some interesting anomalies in the user interface, because what's logical from the users' task point of view may be different from what's logical from the program's functional point of view. You need to spot these problems as early as possible and try to resolve them with the programmers. From a usability perspective, it's much better to change the program than to try to write instructions that explain its functionality to the users.

Flow diagrams can also provide cross-references to task-topic maps (see Figure 4) or to instructions for completing each task or subtask.

Working with use cases and user scenarios

Task analysis may involve developing use cases, user scenarios, and other user task models. Use cases help testers to develop their test cases and software developers to design the user interface. Writers depend upon use cases to understand the user tasks for which they must write help topics.

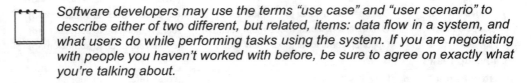

Software developers may use the terms "use case" and "user scenario" to describe either of two different, but related, items: data flow in a system, and what users do while performing tasks using the system. If you are negotiating with people you haven't worked with before, be sure to agree on exactly what you're talking about.

Here is the way I use these terms in this book: use cases and user scenarios describe what an actor (user) should do. They are ideal representations of the user's actions, and don't specify the precise interactions that took place. They include:

- The inputs or prerequisites required. (What information does the user need, or what does the user have to do before starting this task, or what does the system or someone else have to do first?)

- What the user needs to do to accomplish this task. May involve several subtasks, using different dialogs in a sequence.

- What happens afterwards. (What outputs are expected, or what task does this one lead to?)

Use cases should be developed (usually by business analysts) during the early planning stages of a software development project, as part of turning user requirements into functional specifications and software design documents. Technical communicators may be involved at this point in the project, but often they are not. Some companies may not develop formal use cases at all.

User scenarios, like user profiles and personas, can be produced by business analysts, software developers, technical communicators, or others, as early as possible in the cycle.

Writers don't usually include use cases or user scenarios in printed documents or online help, but rather use them in preparing specifications for the documents and help; as the basis for determining a list of the tasks to be documented and a logical sequence for those tasks (for printed documents); and in preparing a map of the required help topics. Writers may also use modified scenarios directly in tutorial or training material.

The main difference between use cases and user scenarios is in the degree of detail. Use cases are often high-level descriptions, often focused on what the system is doing, while user scenarios are detailed descriptions of the specific steps the user must perform to accomplish the tasks. In some cases, user scenarios are done in narrative (storytelling) form, similar to the scenario in Example 7. In other cases, a scenario may be similar in form to a use case, but with specific details (a specific name, for example, instead of the generic "recipient"). Use the approach that suits your requirements best.

JoAnn Hackos and Dawn Stevens (*Standards for Online Communication*, 1997, pages 25-29) suggest this sequence when creating scenarios: "Start with routine tasks. Add exceptions. Focus on users' goals, rather than the tasks performed with tools. Don't get bogged down in low-level tasks [but don't cover only the easy tasks—cover what users need to know to do their job]. Avoid defining tasks in terms that only experts will understand. Turn the scenarios into lists of questions users are likely to need information to answer: How do I...? What is...? What do I do if...? What is an example of...? When should I...? What will happen if...?"

Example 7. Use case and user scenario for an e-mail program

In the following examples, you will note that several variations on "how things work" are possible or probable. For example, there probably are several ways to open a new message window, find the recipient's name in a list, or send the message. The use case does not specify which method is used; some companies might develop a separate use case for each variation of each step.

Use case example

Description: Sending an e-mail message to recipient in address book

Actor: User of e-mail client software

Preconditions:

- E-mail client software must be open.
- Recipient must be in the address book.

Steps and substeps:
1. Open a new message window.
2. Choose recipient from address book.
   [This would have substeps.]
3. Type subject (optional).
4. Type message.
5. Add signature (optional).
6. Click Send.

Outcomes: Message is queued for sending or is sent immediately.

Exceptions: What to do if the name isn't in the address book

Related tasks and use cases:
- Add name to address book
- Check spelling in message
- Queue messages for sending
- Send queued messages
- Send message immediately without queuing

User scenario example

Jean Weber wants to send an e-mail message to her editor, Tamar Granor.

Jean's e-mail software is open, so she clicks the New Message icon on the toolbar to open a new message window.

Jean double-clicks in the "To:" field to open the address book. Her address book entries are arranged in "Last name, First name" order, so she presses **G** to jump to the appropriate part of the list, scrolls down until she finds "Granor, Tamar" and then double-clicks on that name.

The system returns Jean to the New Message window, where Tamar Granor's e-mail address now appears in the "To:" field.

Jean presses the Tab key to move to the "Subject:" field and types a subject for her message. She then clicks in the message-text portion of the window and types her message.

When she is finished, she clicks the Send icon on the toolbar. The message is queued for sending. In this case, Jean must be sure to send the queued messages later.

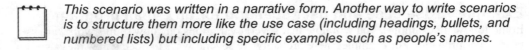 *This scenario was written in a narrative form. Another way to write scenarios is to structure them more like the use case (including headings, bullets, and numbered lists) but including specific examples such as people's names.*

What questions will the audience ask?

To help you determine what topics should be covered in the online help, use the user profiles, task lists, use cases, and user scenarios to help imagine what questions the audience might ask, beyond "what do I put in this field?" or "How do I use this dialog box?"

Especially when there is no printed manual, online help must include enough conceptual information to answer questions like "Does this program do X?" or "How can I do X using this program?" so users can find the parts of the program they need.

When compiling lists of questions, remember that users often think of terms that aren't used in your product. For example, they might say "search" when your product uses the term "find," or they may be trying to "format" a paragraph but the program uses the term "style."

Think of questions that might be asked by novice, intermediate, and experienced users. Remember, no question is too stupid—what's obvious to you and the software developers may be totally incomprehensible to some of the users, who may be used to a different way of doing the same task using another program.

Think of expectations the users may have—for example, from prior experience with competitors' products or other software used in your company if you're dealing with an in-house product.

Think of tasks that involve more than one window or dialog in the software. In the scenario given earlier, Jean used both the New Message window and the Address Book window to accomplish one task.

Does the help need to cover any tasks that aren't done using the software, but are essential to the sequence of software tasks? For example, an in-house system is probably designed to fit in with specific workflow requirements in the company; in this case, a few words about that workflow might be very helpful to some users, such as new hires or people transferred into a new job. For example: "Information for the fields in this window comes from the printed XYZ form that you received from Marketing."

You might also need a glossary of terms used specifically at a company, if they use common words to mean something different from the usual meaning. For example, does the word "part" mean a customer's part that they are building, or a component used to create a customer "assembly"?

Build lists of users' questions and help topic types

From the task and questions lists, you can begin building lists of users' questions and help topic types. These lists form the basis of the writer's help topics and the index and table of contents. They will evolve as the project progresses.

Figure 3 (adapted from Deaton and Zubak, *Designing Windows 95 Help*, 1996) shows an example of a spreadsheet used to map help topics to a task list. You could add other columns to the spreadsheet.

User task	Associated help topic	Topic type	Links to
Task A	Topic title or ID number. You could split this into two or more rows, because several topics could be associated with one user task.	For example, conceptual, procedural, glossary, field-level.	List other topic IDs that this topic links to, including pop-ups.
Task B			
Task C			

Figure 3. Example of a spreadsheet used to map help topics to a task list.

Example 8. Part of a task-topic list for TreeLine

Taking the information in Figure 2, you can develop a task-topic list for TreeLine. A small excerpt from such a list is shown in **Figure 4**. The names of the help topics shown in the second column may not be the final topic titles, but they should indicate to the writer what information belongs in them.

User task	Associated help topic	Topic type	Links to
Set up nodes for organizing information	How to create a node	Procedural	What is a node? How to add information Node types Formatting nodes Field help for Create Node dialog
	What are nodes and why do I want to use them?	Conceptual	All topics about nodes Node types Formatting nodes
	Organizing information	Conceptual	All topics about nodes and input of information
Move/copy a node	How to move/copy a node	Procedural	What is a node? Field help for Move/Copy Node dialog
Input information	How to add information	Procedural	How to create and move nodes Organizing information Field help for Add Data dialog
Output information	Types of output and formats	Conceptual	How to output information Field help for Data Output dialog
	How to output information	Procedural	Types of output and formats Field help for Data Output dialog

Figure 4. Part of a spreadsheet mapping help topics to the TreeLine task list.

Conclusion

From the range of techniques for audience and task analysis available, choose those which suit your project's complexity and the level of detail required. Map tasks to help topics as more information becomes available. Use placeholders until you can get the information you need. Always try to see things from the users' perspective.

Updates and corrections to this chapter can be found on Hentzenwerke's Web site, **www.hentzenwerke.com**. Click "Catalog" and navigate to the page for this book.

Chapter 3
Developing Specifications

High-level specifications should include the help format, information types, topic types, navigation and accessibility aids, media types, and other presentation factors; how the help is linked to the application; how the help coordinates with any other documentation for the software; and the tools to be used in developing the help. Detailed specifications get into the specifics of writing conventions, terminology, design and layout, the navigation scheme, and the content of various topic types; they usually include a style guide for the project.

Specifications for online help are a vehicle to communicate your help design to other project members such as developers, marketing personnel, and clients. They are also a guide for the writers during help development.

Include the specifications in your help plan, and be sure to get approval from other stakeholders, such as the client and the application developers.

This chapter summarizes the questions that specifications should answer. It does not address each issue in detail, but provides checklists of issues you should consider. Refer to Appendix A, "Sample Plans and Specifications," for a more detailed treatment of many of these topics.

Consider developing your specifications as a help file that demonstrates the look and feel you intend to provide in the help system itself.

You can download templates for high-level specifications (highlevelspecstemplate.rtf) and detailed specifications (detailedspecstemplate.rtf) from the Hentzenwerke Web site.

High-level specifications

Develop your high-level specifications during the planning stage of the project. Include your decisions in the help plan. High-level specifications should include decisions on these questions:

- How will the online help coordinate with other user documents?
- What type of help will best fit the application?
- How will the help be connected to the application?
- What media types are required?
- What tools are needed?
- What information types and levels are required?
- What topic types are required?
- How will the help windows (or pages) be presented?

- What navigation aids will be used?
- How will the help meet localization criteria?
- How will the help meet accessibility criteria?

How will the online help coordinate with other user documents?

Online help is usually one part of a user documentation set for an application. Help should therefore be planned as part of that set, not in isolation. Here are some issues to consider:

- Is this an in-house software product that will support a set of company procedures? Or is it a more general product that can be used for a variety of purposes?

- Will the application have printed user documentation? What will that be? Some possibilities are a user guide, a quick-reference card, a reference manual, a getting-started guide, and a printed tutorial.

- Will the application have other online documents (for example, a user's guide or reference manual) in addition to the online help?

- Will users be likely to have personal copies of any printed documentation?

- Will different groups of users prefer online or print information? If so, should certain information types go only in one form or the other?

Users of in-house software products may best be served by having dialog-level or field-level online help in addition to other online materials such as a tutorial, a procedures manual, or a reference manual. You can link between these various files, so that users can choose the level of detail that best serves them at a particular time.

You may decide that duplicating some or all of the information in different formats is the best way to serve the users' needs, or you may decide that some information should be in one format only.

If you decide to duplicate information, and different writers are responsible for the different formats, you will need to closely coordinate the writing to ensure consistency of information.

Do you plan to single-source your documentation?

The term *single-sourcing* usually refers to the practice of maintaining one file from which you create printed documents (including those shipped as PDF files), online books (in various formats), and online help. Although single-sourcing is not difficult technically, the results are frequently not as usable as they could be. Writers can prepare usable single-source material, but they often don't.

A full discussion of single-sourcing is outside the scope of this book. The main issue is the way in which writers chunk, sequence, and link information. For example, material intended to be read in a linear sequence may not make sense when topics are read out of sequence, and the number of cross-references appropriate in help is rarely necessary and often intrusive in printed material. If writers intend to single-source, they must plan for the differences between print and online presentation and allow time for the extra work required.

What type of help will best fit the application?

Several types of online help are available, and new variations keep appearing as Web-based applications are developed. You'll need to choose the most appropriate system for your application and your audience, while attempting to plan ahead for changes in technology. See Appendix B, "Help Types and Tools," for more information. Here are some issues to consider:

- Is the application browser-based, Windows-based, designed for some other operating system (such as Macintosh or Linux), or for a product that has specific presentation requirements?

- If the application is browser-based, what variety of HTML-based help do you need? Will all of your users have the same browser, or will you need to design a browser-independent help system?

- If the application is Windows-based, do you want WinHelp, HTML Help (Microsoft's proprietary version), some other HTML-based help, Flash Help, or some other cross-platform format (perhaps looking ahead to porting the application to a non-Windows system)?

- If the application runs on some other operating system, what help system should you choose? You'll need to look at the available systems and tools for that environment.

How will the help be connected to the application?

You need to make sure that you and the programmers agree on how they are going to code the links between the software and the help topics, so that you can plan your help topics and the navigation between them. Document the decisions you make, and the reasons for those decisions, so that later on people don't change things without understanding the consequences. Here are some issues to consider:

- What limitations does the application's user interface place on the types of help access you can make available?

- Will the help be embedded (see "Providing embedded help" in Chapter 8, "Meeting the Needs of Novices to Experts"), or connected at the window (or Web page) level, or will any request for help always start at the contents page or index?

- Will field-level help be provided? How? Possibilities vary with the type of help, but may include rollovers (also called "mouseovers"), tooltips, and pop-up boxes.

- If the programmers say they intend to provide "context-sensitive" help, what do you and they mean by that term? Linking at the page/dialog level or the field level?

- For dialog-level help, will the developers reuse dialogs in a variety of situations, but provide only one link from each dialog to the online help? Or will they provide separate links to the help depending on the version of the dialog in use? From a usability point of view, it is better for the help topics to be written for each situation in which the dialog is used, but this may not be practical for the programmers.

- If some dialogs have tabbed pages, is it possible to link each page individually to a separate help topic? It is easier for the programmers to link the whole dialog, but often better for the users to have separate help topics for each tab.

- Do you need one compiled help file or several files? Many software products are modular; that is, customers may install or have access to a subset of the full product. If the various modules are provided as separate executable files, it will probably be best if the help is also provided in separate files, corresponding to the program files. (You can maintain the help as a single system, but output subsets into compiled files.)

- Are there any other issues you should consider, such as anything unusual about the application that would affect the way the help is accessed from it?

- How much time and what resources are available? You may need to modify, or at least prioritize, your list of preferred help types.

See Chapter 9, "Linking from Application to Help," for more ideas.

What media types are required?

Will your help be mainly text, or will it include graphics (with or without hotspots), animated graphics (such as Flash), video, or audio? You need to answer this question fairly early in the planning process, because the answer will affect decisions on what tools to use. Here are some issues to consider.

Your audience

- What's best for the audience? Will they benefit from the inclusion of multimedia? Is it essential, a nice-to-have feature, or perhaps unnecessary?

- What sort of equipment do your users have? Desktop computers with large monitors, large hard disks, fast CD-ROM drives, high-speed Internet connections? Or are they using older laptops in the field, with no convenient way to carry a CD with them and no convenient Internet access?

- If the application is Web-based, will users be accessing the help over the Web? Will they all have high-speed connections? Will graphics and multimedia slow down loading or use of the help enough to be a problem for users?

The writing team

- If new tools are required, you'll need to purchase them and the writing team will need to learn how to use them. Training might be required; is training in your chosen tools available in your area? Buying and learning new tools take time and money, which you must take into consideration when planning the help. You might need to modify your plans if the resources aren't available.

- If multiple media types are planned, and the tools used will support them all, should the writing team specialize according to their proficiency in a particular medium? For example, would one person be responsible for all the video?

What tools are needed?

Here are some categories of tools that you may need for the project, in addition to a suitable computer and monitor. See Appendix B, "Help Types and Tools," for more information.

Hardware

- Audio recorder
- Video camera
- Digital camera for still photos
- For Web applications, a modem and dial-up line for testing
- Different sizes and resolutions of monitors, including laptops, for testing

Software

- Help authoring
- Screen capture (static)
- Screen camera (software for recording motion pictures)
- Graphics
- Indexing
- Editing and reviewing
- Change tracking
- Library management
- For Web applications, a range of browsers for testing purposes
- If relevant, computers with different operating systems, for testing purposes

Do some research before choosing software. Some considerations to keep in mind are:

- How stable is the software? (The latest version of a tool may not be the best choice for a production environment.)

- What workarounds will you need for any of the software limitations?

- Do help-authoring tools have the editing, tracking, and reviewing features you need, in addition to help-development features?

- Are writers familiar with the software or will they need to learn how to use it?

You can find out a lot about the suitability of software by:

- Using it, or an evaluation copy, to create some representative samples of the help.

- Asking questions on a users' group forum (see Appendix C, "For More Information"), to find out others' experiences with the software on similar projects.

What information types and levels are required?

Online help may include four general information types:

- Conceptual
- Procedural
- Reference
- Instructional (for example, tutorials)

Each information type can include several topic types, as described in "What topic types are required?" later in this chapter.

As discussed in Chapter 2, "Analyzing Audiences and Tasks," audiences (users) vary in their knowledge, skill levels, and other characteristics. Your audience analysis should indicate which users you need to cater to.

You may not need to include all combinations of users' knowledge and usage. A good way to help you decide is to develop a table relating the types of users to the types of information. In the table, write down what topics would best serve each combination. Some possibilities are shown in **Table 1**. The mix might be quite different for your application and audience.

Table 1. *This example of the types of information to be provided for different audiences demonstrates how help can serve a variety of needs.*

	Novice user	Expert user	Occasional user
Conceptual help *abstract ideas*	Overviews; what you can do and which parts of the application to use for what task	How it works	Overviews
Procedural help	Detailed steps to accomplish a task, using specific fields on each window	What application windows to use, or summaries of steps	Summary of steps to accomplish a task
Reference help	Lookup tables for help in selecting codes, filling in fields	Details and examples of how to choose parameters	Memory-joggers and lookup tables
Instructional help	Basic tasks	Probably not required	More likely to need performance support material

What topic types are required?

As you probably realize, topic types and information types overlap considerably. Just as different applications and users require different mixes of information types, they also require different mixes of help topic types.

This section describes some of the types of help topics. Choose the topic types that are appropriate for your application and audience.

 The names given to the topic types in this section are for convenience only. They do not appear in the online help itself, and other sources of information may call them by different names.

Overviews and conceptual topics

Brief description of the application's purpose, intended use, and most common or important tasks; fundamental concepts, components or actions in an application; the theory, logic or reasoning behind a task.

Window- or dialog-level topics

Brief description of what a particular window does and how it works. Generally linked to one or more procedural topics.

Procedural (task) topics

Step-by-step instructions (usually numbered) on how to complete a task. Often called directly from a dialog.

Field-level topics

Brief explanation about a part of the interface (individual fields and controls within a window). May appear in a pop-up box or "tooltip."

Reference topics

Explains detail beyond the "how to" level, such as command structure and options, keyboard shortcuts, and so on. Usually non-procedural. Generally aimed at more expert users.

Lookup topics

Codes, values, variables, parameters, or other data needed when filling in a report, making a calculation, or quoting a price. Useful when the user interface does not include drop-down lists of these values.

Example topics

Illustrate expected results when the user has followed some procedure; for example, some sample code or a picture of a dialog box with the correct options selected.

Problem-solving topics

Lists of common problems with the software, with procedures and recommendations for diagnosing and solving the problems.

Frequently Asked Question topics

Answers to common questions that users may have when working with the application.

Glossary and other pop-up topics

Brief explanations of terms, provided as pop-ups. You can also gather glossary definitions into a single topic, organized alphabetically, that users can browse. Consider putting a Glossary button or tab on the Help window, or a Glossary option on the Help menu.

Error message help topics

Assistance for system messages that appear on the interface. Describe what's happening, how to respond, and the consequences of the user's choices. If possible, the message itself should provide enough information so this type of help isn't required; but if the choices are complex, message help may be necessary.

Tip-of-the-day topics

Brief hints and tips on how to use the software, usually provided so a new tip appears each time the program is started. Be sure to provide a way for users to turn off this feature.

Wizards, coaches, and other performance support topics

Usually provided for less-experienced users, to guide them through typical tasks. After the user has entered the required information, or selected from the choices provided, the wizard or coach processes the information. Advanced users often prefer to skip the wizards and do the tasks directly.

Show-me, demonstration, and tutorial topics

Usually provided for less-experienced users, to guide them through typical tasks. These topics differ from wizards by not collecting task information from users, but merely demonstrating how to do something (for example, where to find a particular command in the menu structure). Demonstrations may include simulations or digital video, often created using screen camera software.

How will the help windows (or pages) be presented?

The answer to this question depends on an understanding of the audience's expectations and preferences, in addition to any constraints imposed by the help system you're using. Some issues to consider:

- What should be the default help presentation? Always on top, beside the application window, embedded, or other?

- What size will the default help window be?

- Will the table of contents be visible alongside each help topic?

- Will you include tooltips or secondary and pop-up help windows in addition to primary help windows?

- Will you use JavaScript, dynamic HTML (DHTML) or other scripting/programming techniques to display the table of contents, index, help windows, or customized help?

- Will individual users be able to:
  - Change the font size and typeface?
  - Change the help window size?
  - Hide or show the table of contents and index?
  - Print the entire help file, individual topics only, or none?
  - Bookmark topics?
  - Annotate topics?

JavaScript is not the same thing as Java, despite the similarity in names. Java is a full programming language used to write browser-based applications. JavaScript is a simple scripting language used by HTML authors to write functions. When talking with software developers, be sure you use the correct term.

What navigation aids will be used?

Although many people will look only at the help topic that appears when they request help from an application window (and others will never look at the help at all), you need to provide a variety of clear, easy-to-use navigation aids to enable readers to move around in the help file, find what they want, and not get lost. Navigation aids include:

- Keywords (index entries)
- Table of contents
- Search facility
- Browse sequences
- Visual aids such as icons
- Buttons with words, or text-only links
- Cross-references within text
- "Related topics" or "See also" links
- History facility
- Bookmarks and Favorites

Some principles of good navigation aids:

- The help should be compatible with (although not necessarily the same as) the look and feel of the application. Consider how you will use color, and whether you want to include icons and other design elements.

- Consider your users' expectations about the use of color, icons, topic types, navigation aids, and the placement of information on the screen. For example, if you are writing help for a Windows application, your users may be most comfortable if your help topics look like the help provided by other Windows applications. Conversely, users moving to your application from another platform or a competitor's product may prefer help in a form that is more familiar to them. Ask typical users about their preferences before deciding.

- Be consistent in the placement of navigation aids, so users know where to look for them; for example, at the top or bottom of a page, or on the left-hand or right-hand side. Consider using the same navigation style as the user interface, or look at examples of competitors' products or other applications on the same platform. For in-house products, you might want your help to have the same appearance as other applications used by the staff.

Refer to Chapter 7, "Providing Navigation and Context," for more information.

How will the help meet localization criteria?

Products intended for an international market will probably be translated into other languages. In some countries—for example, Canada—more than one language is a legal requirement. Even if the product and its documentation are provided in only one language, some localization may be necessary if it's being used in more than one country. For example, accounting software distributed in the UK, USA, Australia, and New Zealand may need to consider different accounting terminology or tax regimes.

Localization of products and the accompanying documentation may involve two things:

- Translation into other languages
- Changes to account for regional differences

Regional differences include:

- Weights and measurements
- Date formats
- Temperature scales
- Paper size
- Currencies and formats
- Legal requirements
- Local contact information
- Cultural differences

Some differences can be handled by using appropriate terms when writing; these terms should be included in the project style guide. Others—for example, legal requirements and local contact information—may require the use of conditional text, so several variations of the help system can be produced from one source file.

How will the help meet accessibility criteria?

The audience for most products includes people with a wide range of visual and other physical disabilities, or who may be using a variety of computers and related hardware. Whenever possible, use features that can be used or customized by as wide a range of people as possible. For example:

- Provide multiple access methods for online help (keyboard, mouse).

- Allow users to specify the font and font size to use when viewing help.

- Provide alternatives to graphics that contain information, by including the same information in text above, below, or beside the graphic, or (for Web-based help) as text that appears when the graphic is not displayed or when the user moves the mouse over the graphic.

- Choose colors carefully, considering both users' vision (color blindness) and monitor capabilities (particularly on older laptop computers). Even better, don't specify colors; let the help system use the system-wide colors the user has specified.

You may be legally required to meet certain accessibility criteria, but even if you aren't, doing so can improve all users' experience of the help system, and (for a commercial product) you might help increase sales by making it possible to sell the application to, for example, government agencies. For details on solutions to issues related to Web pages, see the Web Accessibility Initiative and Web Design Group materials (listed in Appendix C, "For More Information"). The guidelines are also usually applicable to online help.

Detailed specifications

Develop your detailed specifications during Step 3 of the planning stage of the project. Be sure to get approval from other stakeholders, such as the client and the application developers.

Detailed specifications for the online help should include:

- Related documents
- Writing conventions
- Terminology
- Design and layout
- Help navigation scheme
- Content of topic types
- Project-specific style guide

Refer to Chapter 10, "Copyediting and Production Editing," and Appendix A, "Sample Plans and Specifications," for more information.

Related documents (primary sources)

List documents containing relevant information that is not repeated in the specifications; for example:

- Company style guide
- Preferred dictionary
- Preferred Web writing guide and/or help writing guide
- Project-specific style guide
- Terminology list

Writing conventions

If you already have documents (such as a style guide) covering writing conventions, you can refer to them in your specifications instead of repeating the information. Be sure to cover such issues as:

- Making topics that stand alone (because you don't know the sequence in which users will read them), though linked to related information

- Topic length, which may vary with the topic type and user type

- How many links are too many for users to find the information they require

- Layering approaches, to provide different levels of detail for different audiences—for example, the use of related topics and hypertext links to provide users with choices regarding what information they want to read

- When to use pop-ups—for example, for brief topics such as glossary items (definitions of terms), field descriptions, and other *brief* explanatory material

- Any consistency issues between the help, the user interface, and the printed documentation

Terminology

If you already have documents covering terminology conventions—for example, the project style guide—you can simply refer to them in your specifications. See Chapter 10, "Copyediting and Production Editing," for more information.

Make sure that terminology, spelling, and capitalization used in the help match those used in the user interface and the printed documentation.

If the application is likely to be translated into other languages, you may need to develop or follow guidelines for limited English.

 Create a terminology list, including terms used by your competitors but not in your product, so you can include relevant synonyms in the index of the help and in the printed user documentation. The terminology list can also form the basis of a glossary and the definitions provided to the translators.

Design and layout

If you already have documents covering design and layout conventions, you can simply refer to them in your specifications. Be sure to cover such issues as:

- Default typefaces and type sizes

- When to use bold or italic type

- When to use colored text, backgrounds, or highlighting

- Paragraph formatting (for example, text flush left, how much space between paragraphs)

- No use of heading numbering in online help

- General style guidelines for numbered, bulleted, and definition lists

- When to use or avoid tables; wide tables in particular are a problem, because of the need for horizontal scrolling

- Table formatting; for example, borders, type size, highlighting (such as bold) for column and row headings

- When to use graphics, and guidelines for size, colors, limited palette, other attributes; test to determine any problems—you may need to change tools or methods

- Whether to use screen captures; if so, what resolution and number of colors to use, and what color palette; whether to use partial captures; whether to use clickable regions (image maps)

- When or if to use non-scrolling regions, frames, or other layout devices—for example, to contain the navigation buttons

- Guidelines for graphics and icon usage if the application is likely to be translated into other languages

Help navigation scheme

Describe or diagram how each topic type will link (or not) to other topic types. Your specification could include graphics showing typical application windows and dialogs, annotated to show a typical set of help entries for that window or dialog type, and how the help topics are linked together. (The graphics could be screen captures from the prototype application, or mockups of application windows.) **Figure 1** shows an example of this type of graphic.

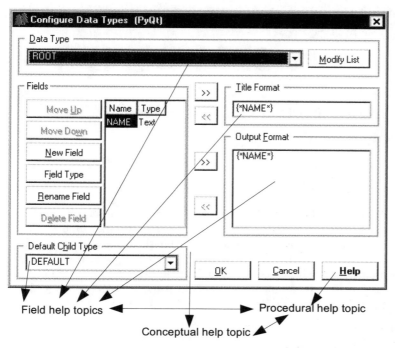

Figure 1. Example of a graphic showing one type of application dialog, the types of help to be associated with that dialog type, and how the help topics are linked.

Content of topic types

In your specifications, include a detailed description of each topic type to be used in the help system, what to include and how to present the material, how the topics are to be accessed from the application, and templates for common topic types. Here are some examples.

Overview topics

Overview topics provide a brief description of the application's purpose and intended use. They may be presented as a single topic (if brief) or as a sequence of related topics.

Users access overview topics through the index, contents page, or links from procedural and other topics. Overview topics cover such issues as:

- Purpose of the application

- Description of changes and new features that will affect users and their work

- Guidance on where users can get help or application support

- How the user can get started with the application (for example, a brief description of the navigation options)

- How the user can get help on the application

- Brief description of the most common or important tasks a user can perform, with links to procedural topics

- Brief description of user roles, if any

Overview topics contain:

- Topic title

- Description or discussion, using bullet points where appropriate

- Links to related topics

See **Figure 2** for a sample overview topic.

Conceptual topics

Conceptual topics provide information about the work, specific tasks or workflow process, including its purpose, the way information flows through the process, specific outputs produced or tracked within the process, and the people involved in the process. Conceptual topics try to answer questions such as "What is the process?", "Why is it performed?", "Who is involved?", "What is produced?", and "When is information needed?"

Users access conceptual topics through the index, contents page, or links from procedural and other topics. Conceptual topics may cover these issues:

- Present concepts to users

- Provide an overview of the workflow process and task steps

- Provide a general description of the people and roles involved in the process

- Discuss business processes or rules

- Describe end products that users create when using the application

- Describe objects or resources that users work with during the business process

- Discuss how to get started using the application

- Share useful working tips

Conceptual help topics contain:

- Topic title (phrase in user terms, perhaps as a question)

- A section on the process or object purpose

- A section on how objects fit into the process, or links to procedural help

- Related topics list

See **Figure 3** for a sample conceptual topic.

Title of help topic	**What's new?**
Brief description of process or purpose	For your convenience, we've assembled these lists of key features, along with ideas about how you might apply them to your work.
Links to related information	**What do you want to read about?** Automating your tasks and getting assistance Creating graphics Working with Web tools Reading online documents Multilingual support

Figure 2. Sample overview topic.

Title of help topic	**Getting started**
Brief description of process or purpose	What you see when you start [product name] depends on how your system was set up when it was installed.
	Most reception setups will display either:
	Patient Search window
	Today's Patient List window
	You can select a patient from either of these windows, then click the appropriate button to perform various tasks such as billing, receipting, account inquiry, and so on.
Links to procedural help	Selecting a patient
Links to related information	**Related topics**
	The parts of the [product name] window
	Patient Search window
	Today's Patient List window

Figure 3. Sample conceptual topic.

Dialog-level topics

Dialog-level topics provide information on how to use the active window or dialog, a description of tasks that can be accomplished with the dialog, and details on dialog elements and processing.

Dialog-level topics are displayed when the user presses F1 or a Help button on an application window or dialog. In some cases dialog-level help will be combined with procedural help—for example, when a single sentence or brief paragraph is sufficient to describe the dialog. Dialog-level help topics contain:

- Window or dialog title

- Brief overview of what the user can do in the window. When writing the overview:

  - Focus the description on why users would want to use the dialog and how it will help them complete their work.

  - Keep the explanation brief, because dialog-level help is meant to be a memory jogger rather than a tutorial. If a longer explanation is necessary, link to a conceptual topic.

  - Do not describe anything beyond the current application window unless this window must be used in a specific sequence and you need to refer to other windows as a result.

- ▪ Describe what the user can do in the specific parts of the dialog, if the interrelationship between the components of the dialog would not be obvious from the field-level or procedural help for the dialog.

- (optional) Processing rules

- Procedures for the tasks a user can perform with the window, or links to them

- (optional) Links to pop-up descriptions of fields, push buttons, and other controls (if you have decided to include this information in dialog-level topics)

See **Figure 4** for a sample dialog-level help topic.

Title of help topic	**Customer Inventory – Orders page**
Brief description of what the user can do	Use the **Customer Inventory – Orders** page to search for, view, and add customer order details.
Instructions on how to get more information about fields and controls	**What's on this page?** Click on the window elements and press **F1** to get more information.
Links to procedural help	**How do I use this page?** Adding a customer order Checking a customer order Searching for records Adding a new record
Links to related information	**Related topics** Items Ordered pane Processing customer orders

Figure 4. Sample dialog-level help topic.

Procedural ("how to") topics

Procedural topics provide step-by-step instructions on how to complete a user task. User tasks often involve the use of more than one window or dialog box.

Users access procedural topics through the index, contents page, or links from window- or dialog-level topics. Procedural topics contain:

- Task title (briefly identifies and describes the task procedure)
  - Phrased using terms that are familiar to users; users should be able to predict whether the topic matches their task goals just by reading the title
  - Begins with the gerund form of a verb (ending in –ing; for example, Submitting), followed by an object
- Purpose of task or procedure from the user's perspective (a sentence or two that explains the task purpose, its usefulness, and the expected outcome or result)
  - Explains, in the users' own language, why they would want to perform this task and how it relates to their work; focuses on user needs, not on how the application works
  - Answers questions like "What user problem does the procedure solve?" and "How does the procedure fit into the user's work?"
- Prerequisite conditions or tasks that users must perform before beginning this task
  - If the prerequisite tasks have procedures of their own, link to help topics for those tasks
- Step-by-step instructions or procedures (numbered steps that describe how to complete the task)
  - Begins with an infinitive tag—a short phrase beginning with "To"; for example, "To submit the form:", "To change an emergency contact:". The infinitive explains the purpose of the steps that follow.
  - Each step describes a single action, such as clicking a button, selecting an item, choosing a menu item, or typing text in a field. It is written as a verb followed by a noun phrase.
  - If there are multiple ways to complete an action, document a single approach and choose the approach that users will easily understand and learn. Provide cross-references to other topics that describe alternative ways to complete the action, but don't provide cross-references for common actions.
  - Procedural topics typically contain about 5 or 6 steps. If a procedure starts to exceed 8 steps, consider breaking it into two procedural topics.
- What happens now? What happens after a user performs the task steps (outcome; results and follow up information)?
- Related topics list

See **Figure 5** for a sample procedural topic.

Title of help topic	**Adding a customer**
Purpose	To add a customer record:

Steps	1. Open the **Customer Maintenance** dialog by clicking a **Customer** button from any dialog.
	
	2. Type the relevant details about the customer in the **Customer Contact**, **Customer Address** and **Account Manager** sections.
	
	3. You must fill in the following fields:
	
	   • Customer Name (the full company name of the customer)
	   • Customer Contact section: First Name, Last Name, Phone
	   • Customer Address section: Street Number, Name, Type, Town, State, Post Code
	
	You may also fill in any other details in the relevant fields.
	
	4. Save the record by clicking the **Save** button on the toolbar.

What happens now?	When you save the record, [product name] automatically assigns the **Cust ID** to the customer.
Related topics	**Related topics** Changing customer records Deleting customer records

Figure 5. Sample procedural topic.

Field-level topics

Field-level topics answer the question, "What is this and why would I want to use it?" For entry fields, these topics also answer the question, "What do I type here and what restrictions are there on how I enter the information?"

Users access field-level topics through links from procedural and other topics, or by positioning the cursor in a field and pressing F1, or through the "What's this?" function (whatever processes have been chosen for your product).

When writing field-level topics:

• Do not include a title, because these are pop-up topics.

• Be brief, and include only essential information.

- For an entry field, include a brief description of the information that should be typed into the field, if it is not obvious.

- If relevant, mention any restrictions such as case sensitivity, limits on numbers of characters, or the format of dates.

- If relevant, include information about why a setting might be disabled and how the user can enable it.

- Do not include a Related Topics list.

- If relevant, make these lookup topics, as described later in this chapter.

See **Figure 6** for two samples of field-level topics.

Sample 1

> The Family Search button opens a Search window containing the names of patients associated with this family. Select a name and click OK to return to this window with the fields filled in with the selected patient's details.

Sample 2

> You can use up to 12 characters (uppercase and lowercase letters, numbers, spaces, hyphens, etc.) in the First Name field. Type the name exactly the way you want it to appear. For example:
>
> David
> LaVerne
> Mei-Lin

Figure 6. Sample field-level topics.

Problem-solving topics

Problem-solving topics provide lists of common problems with the software, and include procedures and recommendations for diagnosing and solving the problems.

Users access problem-solving topics from the index, contents page, or links from other topics, including error message topics.

These topics contain:

- Topic title (a statement of the problem)

- Diagnostics list or matrix, if required, with links to solutions (may be part of one topic, or separate topics)

- Solution to problem, if it can be provided in one topic

See **Figure 7** for a sample problem-solving topic.

Title of help topic	**Report book does not show required data**
Diagnostics	If the name, location, or content of the database changes, a report book will fail to find the required data items.
	[Product name] provides facilities for recovering from these changes.
	The error message will tell you what has changed.
Links to solution topics	<u>If the name or location of a database has changed</u> <u>If the content of the database has changed</u>

Figure 7. Sample problem-solving topic.

Glossary topics

Glossary topics provide brief explanations of terms. They are often provided as pop-up topics, do not contain links to other topics, and generally do not have a title, although they may include the term at the beginning of the topic.

Users access glossary topics through links from other topics. **Figure 8** shows a sample glossary topic.

Prototype
A draft help system, demonstrating the elements, topic types, links, and other features to be included in the working system. Early prototypes can be on paper; later ones should be working, although they may not contain any real information.

Figure 8. This sample glossary topic pops up when the user clicks on the linked term "prototype" in the text.

Reference topics

Reference topics explain details beyond the "how to" level, such as command structure and options and keyboard shortcuts. These topics are usually non-procedural and are generally aimed at more expert users.

Users access reference topics from the index, contents page, or links from other topics. **Figure 9** shows a sample reference topic.

Title of help topic	**What's installed with [product]?**
Purpose	The following table lists components installed during a typical installation and others available when you select the custom installation. The table also indicates where you can find these components in the setup program.
Details	[table inserted here]

Figure 9. Sample reference topic.

Lookup topics

Lookup topics provide lists of codes, values, variables, parameters, or other data needed when filling in a report, making a calculation, quoting a price, and so forth. These topics are used when the user interface does not include drop-down lists of these values.

Users access lookup topics through links from procedural topics, or by positioning the cursor in a field and pressing F1.

See **Figure 10** for a sample lookup topic.

This code appears between the Dr. and Ref. columns.	
R	Receipt
J	Journal (write off)
M	Medicare or Veterans Affairs
I	Private patients
W	Workers Compensation patients
C	Credit
i	Credited invoice
m	Credited Medicare or Veterans Affairs form
D	Deferred

Figure 10. Sample lookup topic.

Frequently Asked Question topics

Frequently Asked Question topics answer common questions that users may have when working with the application.

These questions typically involve tool-related quirks, such as areas in which the tool behaves differently from other applications or from what users expect. Example questions are:

- Why can't I find the name of a customer in the list?

- Why can't I edit a document?

- Why can't I view a document?

Users access Frequently Asked Question topics from the index, contents page, or links from other topics, including error message topics.

Frequently Asked Question topics contain:

- Title containing the question

- An answer to the question, which may include procedural steps or include a link to an existing procedure

- Related Topics list, if relevant

If the same problem could arise from several sources, include a series of steps to assist the reader in determining just what the underlying problem is, or refer to a problem-solving procedure. These steps are usually best linked to other help topics that discuss what to do for each situation.

Figure 11 shows a sample Frequently Asked Question topic.

Title of help topic: the question	**Why can't I edit a document?**
Answer to the question: a) What the cause may be	• You may not have the proper authority to edit the document. To edit a document, you must have author or editor access to it. This means you must be the owner of the document.
b) What the user can do about it	To learn what level of access you have to a document:

1. Display the workspace by selecting **Window - Workspace**.

2. Click on the **Teamwork Office** tab.

3. Select the **Teamwork Office** database icon.

4. Click the **key icon** in the status bar at the bottom of the screen.

If you do not have the required access authority, see your manager to arrange the required access.

Figure 11. Sample Frequently Asked Question topic.

Error message help topics

Error message help topics provide information on common error messages and recommended solutions; they give additional guidance (beyond what is in the message itself) on how to solve a specific problem. They should be used only when a message does not include the required information—for example, when the solution is too lengthy and complex to include in the error message itself.

Users access error message help topics through links from error messages. Error message help topics contain:

- Actual message title

- Brief explanation of the problem

- Possible solution or pointer to a help source

See **Figure 12** for a sample error message help topic.

Title of help topic	**Save Conflict message**
Brief description of the problem	Either you or another user of the database saved a copy of this document while you were still editing it.
	A Save Conflict message appeared to find out if you would like to save a second copy of the document containing your edits.
What the user can do, and what the consequences are	If you click **Yes** in the Save Conflict message, two copies of the document will appear in the view. One of the documents will be marked with a replication conflict icon and the words [Replication or Save Conflict]. Review both documents, find your changes, and paste them into the original document. You can delete the [Replication or Save Conflict] document once you have updated the original document with your previous changes.
	If you click **No** in the Save Conflict message, you will lose any changes you made to the version of the document that is now open. Click **No** only if you're sure this version contains nothing you want to save.

Figure 12. Sample error message help topic.

Project-specific style guide

Include details of writing and language use in a project-specific help style guide, as described in Chapter 10, "Copyediting and Production Editing." This style guide usually supplements other, more general, style guides used by the writers.

Start to write the project-specific style guide (sometimes called a *style sheet*) while you are developing the detailed specifications for the help.

A first draft of the style guide should be completed before writers start writing, but style guides often continue to develop as questions arise during writing of the first few help topics. For example, you might ask, "What do we call this?" "Is this word capitalized?" "Do we type *in* or *into* a field?" When you decide on answers, record them in the style guide. As each issue is resolved and recorded, the writing becomes more consistent and style-compliant.

Conclusion

Specifications communicate the design of your help system to other project members and act as a guide for writers and editors during help development. Specifications should answer questions about the information types, topic types, navigation and accessibility aids, and media types to be included in the help; how the help should be linked to the application; writing conventions, terminology, design, and layout; and the content of various topic types. You can write specifications early in the product development cycle.

Updates and corrections to this chapter can be found on Hentzenwerke's Web site, **www.hentzenwerke.com**. Click "Catalog" and navigate to the page for this book.

Chapter 4
Prototyping the Help System

You can build a prototype of your help system in several stages. In the early, high-level concept and design prototype, be sure to include examples of all relevant navigational aids, topic types, and links between topics. Later, as you outline and map the help project, you can build a more detailed contents prototype.

Creating a prototype of your help system can save you hours of work later, especially if you need to get management approval for the design.

Plan to build the prototype in two stages: a high-level concept and design prototype and a detailed contents prototype. You may need to get agreement from the client or other stakeholders that each stage of the prototype is acceptable to them.

Your help system may be self-contained or it may include items that are essentially part of the user interface, such as field help that is displayed when users move the mouse pointer over a field or click a link. If you're planning to include this type of help, you'll need to work closely with the software developers to make sure your content works with their program. The prototype stage is when you want to get this working.

Why build a prototype of a help system?

Prototypes are an important part of the planning process. Here are some reasons for building one:

- Problems found at this step are easier and cheaper to fix than problems found later.

- You can test a prototype for usability and fix major problems early, before a lot of writing is done. See Chapter 11, "Usability Testing on a Budget."

- You may have the opportunity to test your help system design in conjunction with the user interface design, to find out if it's compatible from both technical and usability points of view.

- You can develop an early prototype without knowing exactly what the software's user interface looks like. If you're working in any environment where software design specifications are not up-to-date, if the specs change rapidly (as in "agile" programming), or if they aren't communicated clearly to the writers, this up-front work can help you minimize a mad scramble at the last minute.

- If someone else is developing the software for the help system (for example, a Web developer may create the working help system for a Web application), then you can get approval for the design and navigation of the help system before the other person does the working version.

- When you create a working prototype, you'll discover any problems with your help-authoring tool, the skills of the writers using the tool, or the output from the tool. This is the time to get some supplementary training, or decide to modify the design—not when you're in the middle of major writing work.

- Working prototypes can also help you identify any problems writers may have in working with the programmers, so you have a chance to try to negotiate a good working relationship. Many problems aren't technical, but political and managerial.

- Software developers often create prototypes of the software. Your credibility may increase if they see you do the same thing.

- You can identify topics that are common to several tasks, and flag them so you write once rather than duplicating topics—and you can make sure the common topics make sense in all of the situations where they're used.

- If you're planning to incorporate any features such as animation or user customization using scripting, you can test these features to ensure they actually work, before using them in the production system.

- Building a prototype should raise many of the questions that your style guide should answer, so you can develop, change, or confirm the style guide as you discover what works and what doesn't.

- You can turn parts of your prototype into templates for the writers, or incorporate pre-existing templates into the prototype, to improve consistency within the help system. Even if you are the only person working on the help system, you will probably save time and not have to worry about remembering how you did something in a different part of the system.

 People use the term "template" to mean different things, from a reusable design to a set of instructions for the contents of a document. In this book, I'm using the term to mean a combination of the two: both design and contents. Be sure you and others agree on terminology such as this.

Building a high-level concept and design prototype

In the high-level concept and design prototype, you need to include examples of all the types of windows and navigation aids to be used in the help. None of the controls need to work, but you do need to specify what the controls and navigation buttons do.

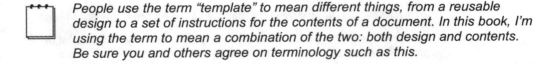 *You can develop an early concept and design prototype before you have the details of the user interface and all its windows and controls. Early help-system prototypes are often developed in parallel with the design and prototyping of the software's user interface.*

Some or all of this step can be drawn by hand on paper or a whiteboard, or by using drawing software to produce printouts or paper mock-ups of the help window designs. An early electronic prototype could be a series of presentation slides or a working series of help windows.

Choose the early prototyping method (paper or electronic) that is most effective and efficient within your work group. You might start with paper and move to an electronic prototype as the design is developed and approved. Involve real users in the evaluation, if you can.

Advantages of paper prototypes

- You don't need any special equipment to create or display paper prototypes, so you can work with them even when you don't have a computer or the required software available. (If necessary, you can fax or scan and e-mail these designs to remote colleagues.)

- Paper prototypes help people focus on the concepts and the logic of the help system from the users' point of view, instead of being sidetracked with software issues. Many help authors get so involved in using tools to produce early designs, that they don't focus enough on navigation and content. Many clients get sidetracked by software issues such as nonworking controls on an early electronic prototype, but they don't expect a button on a printout to be clickable.

- If you include some good sample topics, you can get feedback on how appropriate they are for the target audience.

Advantages of electronic prototypes

- Some people think paper prototypes look "unprofessional," even though they are frequently used by usability consultants and software development teams. If your manager, clients, or coworkers have a negative attitude toward paper, you may need to skip the paper prototype stage. On the other hand, if the software developers use paper prototypes when designing the user interface, you'll fit right in.

- In teams where people don't meet in person, you may need to have the prototype in some electronic form. You can scan your paper designs and fax or e-mail them, or send hard copies, but you might find that creating an electronic prototype from the start is more efficient.

- If you include some good sample topics in context (such as field help), you can get feedback on how well they work technically. For example, very long "tool tip" text is a poor use of that technique and should be displayed some other way.

- You can determine whether some features actually work—for example, the script you wrote to allow user customization, or an animation technique to be used to explain a difficult concept.

What to include in a high-level prototype

You don't need much real information about the product at this point, but you do need the task list from Chapter 2, "Analyzing Audiences and Tasks." Include examples of the design and navigation system and at least one example of each topic type, with all relevant navigation aids, links between topic types, and other design components such as scripts and animation.

Design and navigation

As a starting point, use the design and layout, help navigation scheme, and content of topic types defined in the detailed specifications (see Chapter 3, "Developing Specifications").

 If you produced the help specifications as a working help system, you have already done part of the concept-and-design stage of prototype development.

If your help system uses a standard presentation layout such as Microsoft's HTML Help, you won't need to do much more than show a sample screen. However, even HTML Help has author-definable options (such as which buttons appear in the top navigation bar; whether the help opens with the side navigation—Contents, Index, Search, and other tabs—showing or hidden; and what tabs are found in the side navigation), so your sample screen needs to show exactly what users will see. (See **Figure 1**.)

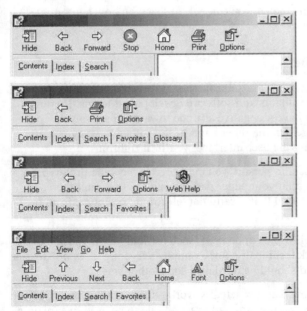

Figure 1. Examples of top and side navigation bars for HTML Help.

If the help system will be displayed within the same navigation framework as the application itself (as some Web sites do), you also won't need to do much more than show a sample screen (see **Figure 2** and **Figure 3**).

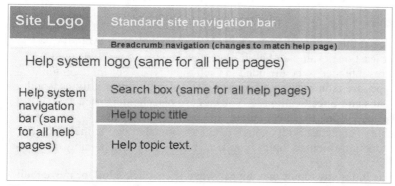

Figure 2. *Example of an early design prototype for a Web site's help system, showing screen areas as blocks of color.*

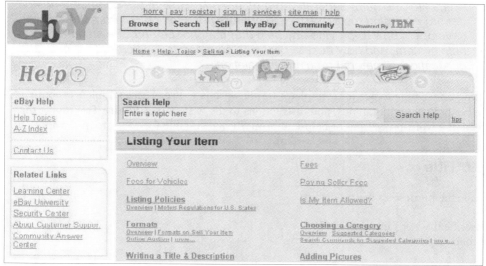

Figure 3. *Example of an early design prototype showing more detail, with areas blocked out as in Figure 2. I've used a screen capture from eBay (http://www.ebay.com/) to simulate the early design, which could have been produced as a picture using a graphics package.*

If you're being more creative in your help-system design, you need to show the design in more detail in your prototype. In that case, you might produce the first iteration of the design and navigation prototype as a hand-drawn diagram or series of diagrams showing different topic types. After discussion, you might produce a second iteration using a graphics package.

Sample topics

Create some sample topics at this point, if you haven't already created them for the specifications. Include at least one example of each topic type you plan to include, and examples of all the features intended to be included in each topic type. (For more on topic types, see "What topic types are required?" in Chapter 3, "Developing Specifications," and Appendix A, "Sample Plans and Specifications.") You can use placeholders such as "Procedure steps go here" and "Link to concept topic" in your sample topics.

Include a sample table of contents, with enough detail to show that you're including task-oriented topics, not just function-oriented topics (you are, aren't you?), and possibly concept-oriented topics.

If your help system includes any topics that appear when users click a link or move their mouse over a field in the application, you may need to borrow or create some sample application screens in order to demonstrate the use of those help topics.

For translation purposes, it's best to keep all text (for the user interface as well as for the help) separate from other code. How this is done depends on the programming tools used. Help authors need to find out from the software developers how to provide any help that may not be part of a stand-alone help system, and how best to deal with common text, in order to avoid duplication of material requiring translation.

Turn your sample topics into templates for the writers to use. These templates should include boilerplate text, graphics, and instructions to the writers (see **Figure 4**). Provide the templates in a word-processing or help-authoring format suitable for your group's work flow.

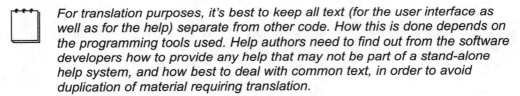

Figure 4. Sample template for a procedural topic.

Create a working high-level prototype

At this point you should create a working electronic prototype using your help-authoring software, to make sure the prototype design works. Here are some suggestions:

- Use the sample topics you created earlier, including the table of contents topic.

- Make sure all the navigation buttons and other controls work as intended.

- Insert working links between topics; create more topics as needed.

- If you're planning to use any browse sequences (described in more detail in Chapter 7, "Providing Navigation and Context"), create some placeholder topics to demonstrate the use of the browse sequence.

- If possible, test the prototype help system with the prototype application software, to see if help topics appear when they should.

When your high-level design prototype is working the way you want, get it approved by your manager or client.

Building a detailed contents prototype

The next step is to produce a detailed contents prototype.

By this time, the detailed software design specifications (and possibly a prototype) should be available, and the programmers should be busy coding and unit testing.

Even if some details of the user interface are expected to change, you can begin outlining and mapping the help project. Start with the high-level task work flow and add granularity (more specific topics, if necessary, or more detail in the topics you plan here) as more details become known.

Outline and map the help project

Topic outlines and maps expand upon the information gathered in the audience- and task-analysis stage (see Chapter 2, "Analyzing Audiences and Tasks") to show:

- Each topic to be included in the help system

- The information type and topic type for each topic

- The audience for each topic

- The relationship between the various help topics and the application dialogs

- The logical organization of topics for the table of contents

- Logical links between topics

You can show these relationships in a table, spreadsheet, or diagram. For most projects, you would use a combination of methods. The major help-authoring tools can produce various types of topic outlines, or you can use database, spreadsheet, or flowcharting software.

Mary Deaton and Cheryl Lockett Zubak cover this topic in detail in Chapter 5 of their book, *Designing Windows 95 Help* (1996). **Figure 5** is adapted from one of their tables, which applies to any help system.

Contents heading	Topic title	Topic ID	Audience	Topic type	Information type
Heading A	Topic Z				
	Topic Y				
	Topic X				
Heading B	Topic W				

Figure 5. Example of a topic outline in spreadsheet form.

Figure 6 shows a planning spreadsheet for context-sensitive help, adapted from Kelly Dodge and Lauren Ward (*Planning and Designing Multi-Authored Help Systems*, 1999).

Dialog, wizard page, or field	Topic title	Topic ID	Context number	Access method
Application item from which help is called	Title of associated help topic	Usually a text string generated by the help-authoring tool	A number provided by the programmers or assigned by the writer	F1, Help button, Help menu item (which one?), or other

Figure 6. Example of a context-sensitive help log, with explanations.

Figure 7 (also from Deaton and Zubak, 1996) shows a task-feature matrix, which lists tasks on one axis and program features on the other. This matrix can help you understand which tasks your users might be performing, and what part of the program they might be using, when they read your help topic. You might not need this level of detail for a relatively small, simple program, but you'll definitely find it useful when writing help for a large, complex program.

User task	Program feature 1	Program feature 2	Program feature 3	Program feature 4	Program feature 5
Task 1	X Notes....				
Task 2		X Notes....		X Notes....	
Task 3			X		

Figure 7. Example of a task matrix. To fill in this spreadsheet, list every task in your user task list. Put a check mark in each column under the feature used in performing the task. Include any notes that may help you understand what users are doing when they read the help topics associated with the task.

Turn your task-topic spreadsheet (Figure 3 in Chapter 2, "Analyzing Audiences and Tasks") into a graphic depiction of the relationships between help topics. This graphic depiction is often called a "topic map," "link map," "topic roadmap," or "information web." An example is shown in **Figure 8**.

You can create a roadmap using software or by hand. I've seen quite large systems designed effectively by using an entire wall as a background for hundreds of sticky notes, each representing one topic, with navigation connections shown by string or thin strips of paper. The sticky notes can be color-coded to indicate different topic types.

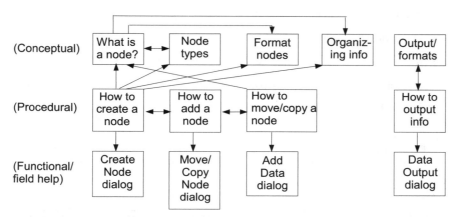

Figure 8. *Sample topic map, derived from the task-topic list for the TreeLine program given in Figure 4 of Chapter 2, "Analyzing Audiences and Tasks."*

 You can set up a topic map without writing the content of any topics. Just create topics and link them in logical ways. You can change topic titles and linking as you refine your prototype, then fill in the contents later.

Here are some hints for successful topic maps:

- Most help projects are too big to be included in a single map. A more typical way to deal with a large project is to create a series of maps or webs, each related to a specific task, group of tasks, or other logical grouping.

- Some topics might be used by several subsets of the help system; you may wish to identify them in some way (such as color-coding) so you don't duplicate those topics.

- Try to avoid grouping by dialog or screen. Grouping by the flow of dialogs is likely to lead to a failure to appreciate how the same dialogs are used in different tasks, or to a tendency to write function-oriented help and forget to include task-oriented help.

Use the outline and roadmap to build a detailed prototype

Use your help-authoring tool to turn your topic outline and map into a detailed prototype or skeleton for your help system. Here are some hints:

- Start with your working high-level prototype.

- Create more topics from your templates.

- Include actual topic titles.

- Create working links between topics in the "Related Topics" sections.

- Create working browse sequences.

- Continue to use placeholders for most details, such as the steps in procedures.

- Make this prototype include all topics you have been able to identify.

- Realize that you'll probably have to make some changes later, so don't expect this iteration to be perfect.

- Test this prototype for usability, even if your only testers are other people on the team. Get real users involved if possible. Tweak the prototype as needed after testing.

 When building hardware, you would normally discard the prototype when you build the real thing. With software, you can expand a prototype into the final system; you don't need to start over.

 A sample working prototype (TreeLinePrototype.zip) is available for download from the Hentzenwerke Web site. When unzipped, the set of HTML files should display in any browser.

Fill in the details

At last! You're ready to start writing. You've reached Step 7, "Write, index, and edit the help topics" from Chapter 1, "Planning an Online Help Project."

I recommend you study Chapter 5, "Avoiding Common Problems," before plunging into the writing.

Conclusion

This chapter has described several techniques for prototyping a help system, even when you don't have many details about the software user interface. Choose the techniques that work for you, but don't skip this step just because you're eager to start writing—a bit of planning now can save a lot of tedious revisions later.

Updates and corrections to this chapter can be found on Hentzenwerke's Web site, **www.hentzenwerke.com**. Click "Catalog" and navigate to the page for this book.

Chapter 5
Avoiding Common Problems

To develop truly helpful online help, writers need to think like potential users, include information to answer their questions at an appropriate level of detail, and make the information easy to find. This chapter describes the 10 most common complaints that users have with online help, the underlying problems that lead to these complaints, and ways to identify the problems and avoid or fix them.

Planners and writers should use this chapter and Chapters 6 through 10 to remind themselves of the types of problems often seen in help systems and how those problems can be minimized or eliminated.

The 10 most common complaints that users have with online help are:

1. I can't find what I'm looking for.

2. I can't figure out what's going on.

3. I can't figure out what will happen when I do something.

4. There's too much detail.

5. There's not enough detail.

6. I can't get to the help when I want it.

7. The program isn't working the way the help says it should.

8. Help says what the system does, but not how to use it.

9. I want a bigger picture of what this program can do.

10. The help is inconsistent and badly written and formatted.

If the creators of a help project have had time to go through planning steps 1 through 6 as described in Chapter 1, "Planning an Online Help Project," they should not encounter many of these problems when they review and test the help. Unfortunately, too many help creators don't go through all the steps, don't have enough time to do them thoroughly, or receive many last-minute changes. If you're reviewing one of those help systems, you can expect to find problems and may not have enough time to review and test thoroughly. Even if you do have time for a thorough review, the writers and programmers probably won't have time to fix all the problems.

 Set up a spreadsheet listing each problem you discover, and the suggested fix. Divide the problems into three categories, as described under "Categorizing problem severity" later in this chapter. Make sure that category 1 problems (serious errors) are fixed before the help ships. Fix as many category 2 problems as possible; you might want to subdivide this group by severity.

1. I can't find what I'm looking for.

This complaint covers a range of problems, so you need to determine what's causing the problem before you can identify an appropriate cure.

Causes

Information not in the help

When you planned the online help, you may have decided not to include some information (for example, because it is in a printed document; or you chose to include only dialog and overview help, but not help for fields and controls). In other cases, the writer may have left out the information by accident.

Help not context-sensitive

Online help systems should have a relevant ("context-sensitive") help topic linked to each application dialog, window, or page.

However, if the help always opens at the table of contents, instead of a relevant topic, users are forced to guess what topic to look up, or they must turn to the index or search function.

Some help systems open to a "what do you want help with" dialog that provides sample choices and a text-entry box, but users may find the choices irrelevant and thus must guess what keywords or question to type in.

Poor table of contents

Topic titles and the structure of the table of contents need to be logical from the users' point of view, which may be quite different from the developers' point of view. A help contents page should be similar to the structure of a table of contents in a printed book.

Poor indexing

All the usual book-indexing questions apply to online help. In addition, help indexes may have a lot of "noise" in them, if writers have allowed their help-authoring tool to construct a draft index, and then have not edited the result. In addition, information may be in the help but not be indexed, so users can't find it.

Poor linking between topics

Any one help topic may answer part of a user's question, but may not be sufficient. Other help topics might answer related questions, but they might not be linked in a convenient or obvious way. Often no links are provided to more general descriptions of tasks or dialogs, even when this information is in the help.

Diagnosing the problem

You already know whether the help opens at dialog-level help or at the contents page. Take some sample questions from your task and question list and try to find the answers, using the index, the contents, and help called from some of the relevant dialogs. Start at any point in the help and try to find related information. For example, using a procedural topic, try to find the associated conceptual help. See if all the necessary information is present—at least something relevant to each question.

Cures

- Identify missing information and decide whether to include it.

- Edit the index and table of contents; see Chapter 6, "Producing the Contents Page and Index."

- Improve linking between help topics; see Chapter 7, "Providing Navigation and Context."

- Include topics for a range of users from novices to experts; see Chapter 8, "Meeting the Needs of Novices to Experts."

- Change linking between dialogs and help; see Chapter 9, "Linking from Application to Help."

2. I can't figure out what's going on.

Common questions, particularly from novice users, often are not answered by help systems:

- How did I get here (to this window, dialog, or page)?

- Where do I go—or what do I do—next? (I'll feel reassured if I know the next step is taking me toward my goal or at least isn't leading me further astray.)

- What does this control do, and should I be using it now? What is its purpose?

- What happens if I choose this option instead of that one?

- Will I be able to recover if my choice is not what I really wanted to do?

Causes

Help topic says only what to do

If context-sensitive help is the default, each topic often tells users only what they can do on a particular dialog, but doesn't say where they came from, where they will go next, or how to decide which choice to make. This can be a particular problem if they're doing something complicated involving a series of steps, and they're not sure if they made a correct choice earlier in the steps.

Writers assume users understand the bigger task

Writers often assume that users already understand how to perform a higher-level task and only need to be told how to operate a particular control, but controls often interact in unfamiliar ways. For example, sometimes you must do A first, then B, but the help doesn't say that. Users often need a bigger picture before they can use a specific control effectively.

Users access help topic from contents or index

Some users will access a topic from the index or contents, often while hunting for a way to do a task. The help may tell them how to do what they want, but not how to get to the part of the application that is described in the help topic. An old assumption was that help should just describe how to use the dialog you are in, because that's all you would want or need to know at that point; you didn't need to be told how to get there, because you already were there. That is not always the case.

Diagnosing the problem

Select topics at random. Ask the following questions:

- Do these topics make sense without prior knowledge of the product or process?

- Do the topics link to other topics, to give a bigger picture? For example, do they link in three directions: to less granular help (more general), to more granular help (where relevant, for example, to fields and controls), and to other related pieces of help?

- Do the topics meet the guidelines for that topic type? (If so, but they are still not adequate, you need to reconsider or redefine the guidelines.)

Cures

- Add a few words to some topics, to clarify the context.

- Improve linking between help topics; see Chapter 7, "Providing Navigation and Context."

- Include topics for a range of users from novices to experts; see Chapter 8, "Meeting the Needs of Novices to Experts."

- Include an overview topic for tasks that require use of different dialogs.

3. I can't figure out what will happen when I do something.

Novice users are often afraid to do something because they don't know what will happen and whether they can recover (roll back) if they make a mistake.

Causes

User interface is unclear

A well-designed user interface should provide enough information for users to determine the consequences of most actions, but if it doesn't, the help must try to compensate for the lack.

In other situations, the interactions between controls may be too complex to describe within the interface. (See problem 2: "I can't figure out what's going on.")

Not enough information is given in the help
The help says what to do but gives no indication of why or what the consequences are.

Writers did not have the information or the time to work it out for themselves
This is a project management problem.

Help specifications were not adequate
That is, the specifications did not call for the type of help that is needed. This is a planning problem, often associated with inadequate consultation between software developers and help developers.

Diagnosing the problem
Use sample tasks and questions you developed at an earlier stage in the project.

- Read random help topics to see if enough information is in them, or if they clearly link to topics that give the necessary information.

- If a working application (or prototype) is available, have someone who has never seen the product attempt to perform the tasks, while referring to the pieces of help that are immediately linked to those dialogs.

Cures

- Tell users what should happen next and what to do if that doesn't happen (provide a link to a problem-solving or other topic; don't dump problem-solving information into a procedural topic).

- Tell users the consequences of different choices (for example, include a table or list of choices and what they do).

- If a choice can't be reversed, be sure to say so up front.

- Improve your guidelines for writing help, if many of the help topics do not address this problem.

See Chapter 7, "Providing Navigation and Context," and Chapter 8, "Meeting the Needs of Novices to Experts," for more information.

4. There's too much detail.
Many users, particularly novices, get lost in too much detail that they don't want, need, or understand. Other users do want and need details, so the writer's job is to make sure the information is there, but doesn't get in the way.

Causes

Writers assume all users need this level of detail
Writers often write for advanced users, who may want or need the detail, or writers believe that all users need to understand the often complex concepts behind an action before they take the action.

Writers don't know how to subdivide information
Inexperienced writers in particular may try to put all relevant information into one topic rather than dividing it into linked topics.

Help tries to cover every alternative
Most software provides several ways to accomplish the same action (from the keyboard or using the mouse, selecting from menus or using toolbar buttons), but help does not need to describe every possibility in each procedure.

One help topic must cover several dialogs
Several dialogs may be derived from the same routine in the program and are linked to one help topic, but they may be sufficiently different that the help topic must be either generalized and vague or long and complex, neither of which meets the users' needs. This is a programming problem as much as a writing problem, and the writer may be unaware of the programming situation.

Diagnosing the problem
Look for:

- Long scrolling topics

- Paragraphs of explanation intermixed with procedures

- Lots of "if–then" branching within a topic

- Several overlapping ideas in one topic, instead of in related topics

- Problem-solving information mixed into procedural topics

Cures

- Split complex topics into several related topics; add relevant links. This cure is especially useful for many examples of "if–then" branching.

- Cut out unnecessary detail, digressions, and explanations, or split into related topics. Think of the way magazine articles put related information into sidebars or boxes, so it doesn't interrupt the flow of the main article.

- Use pop-ups for brief explanations, instead of breaking the flow of the main topic; think of the use of footnotes for this purpose.

- Put the procedure in one topic, background information in another, problem-solving in a third, and so on; add relevant links between all the topics.

See Chapter 8, "Meeting the Needs of Novices to Experts," for more information.

5. There's not enough detail.

When the help includes only the obvious, users complain that the help is too simplified and they need more information or more advanced information.

Not every item needs a long explanation (or, sometimes, any explanation), but if users ask for help, they probably want some guidance, not just a repetition of what's in the field label on the user interface.

Causes

Writers lack information, or are too familiar with the product

With a new product, writers often don't have the necessary details. With revisions, writers are often so familiar with the product that they don't think to include some information; or they don't think any explanation is necessary, perhaps because they assume the user would already know the information.

One window or dialog contains several tabbed pages

If the help for a dialog is the same for all of the tabbed pages, it may be too general and vague or too long and complex.

One help topic covers several dialogs

Several dialogs may be derived from the same routine in the program and are linked to one help topic, but they may be sufficiently different that the help topic must be either generalized and vague or long and complex. The writer may be unaware of the programming situation.

Diagnosing the problem

Have a list of things advanced users might want to know. Can you find the answers? Look for:

- Field help that says no more than the field label says. Ask questions like: "Does it matter in what format this date is entered? If so, what is the correct format? If not, say so!" or "Is this field case-sensitive, and how many characters am I allowed?"

- Remember that many people use words in different ways. Regional and international conventions can vary quite a bit, so include explanations of words that might be used in more than one way. For example, "title" can mean "Mr., Ms., Mrs., or Dr." or it can mean a job title like Manager, which others might call "position."

- Procedures that give no context, explanation, or links to more information.

- No links to introductory, conceptual, or other topics.

- Similar dialogs that arise in different situations (a map or list of the application dialogs is a great help here). Does each dialog have its own explanatory topic, or does one topic cover several dialogs? If the latter, does the help topic make sense in each situation?

Cures

- Include the information if it's not there.

- Add relevant details, but appropriately. If a few words are all that's needed, add them to the topic. If a longer explanation is required, link to a related topic. Write new topics if necessary.

- Link to advanced topics from basic or overview topics; don't clutter basic information with details, but be sure people can find the details if they want them.

See Chapter 8, "Meeting the Needs of Novices to Experts," for more information.

6. I can't get to the help when I want it.

Many users, particularly novices, aren't sure how to get help, or are unaware of the several ways and what the differences are. Even when they do know how to get help, the program may not provide it when they want it.

Causes

Help button or F1 gives an error message or nothing at all happens

This is a worst-case scenario that should be caught by testers; it is usually a programming problem.

No Help button or menu-bar item

Some users may be unaware of alternative ways to get help, or the alternative ways don't work on some dialogs, or a dialog has no help provided, or seemingly trivial dialogs don't have help buttons.

A wizard or other startup window prevents access to the main program

Some programs' default startup sequence includes a wizard to assist users in choosing files or features. However, the wizard may not include enough information to help users understand the choices they need to make. In some cases, users can close the wizard and go directly to the program and the help, but the wizard may not have a clear indication of how to do this. In other cases, closing the wizard closes the program; this situation most commonly occurs when the wizard is intended to lead new users through essential setup information.

Diagnosing the problem

Testing should reveal whether F1 or a Help button does not work, but testers may not be required to determine (a) if each dialog should have help, and (b) if the correct help opens when requested from dialogs that provide it.

Usability tests should indicate where help is needed but is not provided.

Make sure that someone tests the product when it has been connected to the help, to verify that the correct help topic does open.

Cures

Solving these problems may require programming changes.

- Make sure that a relevant dialog-level help topic—not field-level help—is linked to each dialog through F1 as well as through a Help button or menu-bar item.

- Make sure all pages of a wizard have a Help button (if the descriptions on the wizard are not sufficiently self-explanatory, from a naive user's point of view) and an obvious way to cancel the wizard and get to the program's main help files.

See Chapter 9, "Linking from Application to Help," for more information.

7. The program isn't working the way the help says it should.

One of the most frustrating things for users is to look in the help, find what they think is the answer to a question, and then discover that it didn't work. They wonder if they did something wrong, or what else they can do to solve their problem, but often they can't find the answer.

Causes

Late changes to user interface

If the programmers don't tell the writers about changes, the help may not match the program. This is a project management problem.

Inadequate reviews or testing, and writers' lack of knowledge

Often writers do not know about some quirk of the program, usually because they haven't had the time or opportunity to use a complete working system. A common cause is the interaction between controls; if an option is set in one part of the program, it may affect seemingly unrelated choices in other parts of the program. Reviewing and testing should reveal these problems, but reviewers may be too familiar with the system to notice some quirks, and testers often don't examine the contents of help topics.

Diagnosing the problem

Check all procedures against the real program, not the specifications.

- Are any steps left out?

- Do any procedures include things the user might not understand or do correctly—for example, setting specific options in other parts of the program?

- Do any procedures depend on pre-existing conditions or procedures having been done correctly? Is it clear to the user what these are?

- Does the name of every dialog, field, and control match the actual user interface?

- Does the help mention the circumstances under which a control or field is not available, and how to make it available (if that is possible)?

Cures

- Test and edit procedural information and make necessary changes.

- Link from standard procedures to topics on "what to do if XYZ doesn't work."

- Include a problem-solving guide with real diagnostic and cure information in it, not just statements like "see your system administrator."

8. Help says what the system does, but not how to use it.

This complaint is commonly heard about systems developed for in-house use, which are often tightly connected to a defined workflow or the process and procedures within an organization.

A similar complaint relates to more generic software, where a user doesn't know what sequence of steps is necessary to, for example, produce a newsletter or create a graphic.

Causes

Inappropriate user expectations

Users are often unfamiliar with what they are attempting to accomplish, so they can't relate your product to actual work tasks.

Help focuses on low-level tasks

Low-level tasks are usually easy to understand, but don't give clues on workflow or decision making.

Help focuses on what various controls do

Help might not include information on when users might want to use the controls, what relationship the controls have to user tasks, and the conditions under which the controls are not available.

Diagnosing the problem

Use task lists. Attempt to complete a task using the application.

- Can you tell where to start?

- If you need to stop halfway through a task (to go look up some missing information, for example), can you save your work and pick up where you left off later? If not, what are your choices?

- Do low-level task descriptions link to higher-level workflow and "big task" topics?

Cures

Help-system planners must decide how much generic information to include. They may decide that it's not the help system's job to teach people about their field (accounting, graphic design, or whatever), but rather to teach them how to use the program to do their work. Some users, however, won't be familiar with the field; for example, their management may have instructed them to use the product and left them to fend for themselves. Consider these ways to help these users:

- Include some glossary terms or general topics explaining the terminology of your product and its uses and limitations.

- Include some conceptual topics on common tasks users might need to perform. Link the conceptual topics to procedural topics, and make sure the context is clear in all cases.

- Refer users to other sources of information, or link to other information such as the organization's policy and procedures documents (for in-house programs).

- Consider some form of performance support in a future version of the product.

See Chapter 8, "Meeting the Needs of Novices to Experts," for more information.

9. I want a bigger picture of what this program can do.

Many users may be familiar with a similar product, and wonder whether yours can do things they're used to doing. Others may wonder if they're missing out on something, but they don't know what questions to ask. In some cases they know the questions but can't find an answer.

Causes

Some information is only in printed or PDF form

The online help often includes only procedural and system information and not any conceptual or overview information. Although the bigger picture is in the printed (or PDF) documentation, the user may not know that or may not have a copy of the printed or PDF document.

Information is in the help but can't be found easily

The information is there, but it's buried and not revealed by the index or the table of contents.

Information is not available to users in any form

Some products are so lacking in documentation that the only source of information is other users—for example, through online user groups. Open-source and shareware software is particularly subject to this problem; information may be available for programmers, but ordinary users may not understand it or even know it exists.

Diagnosing the problem

Have a list of things that knowledgeable people would know but beginners might not. Are those topics covered somewhere in the help? Can people find them?

Cures

Some possibilities to consider:

- Include "tip of the day" topics (may need programming support).

- Use wizards and coaches (needs programming support).

- Include introductory or tutorial topics.

- Provide overviews, with several levels of detail and links to specific procedures.

- If a printed or PDF book is provided, you could put "look what you can do" information in the book, cross-referenced to and from the help.

- If a printed or PDF book is provided, you could put information in both the book and the help, to assist people who don't have the book available.

- Link between the help and the online manual.

See Chapter 8, "Meeting the Needs of Novices to Experts," for more information.

10. The help is inconsistent and badly written and formatted.

This complaint covers a wide range of writing and formatting problems that should be examined during copyediting. For example:

- Misused or inconsistently used bulleted or numbered lists

- Long, wordy sentences or paragraphs that should be turned into lists

- Poor organization of material within topics and between topics

- Unclear or misleading topic titles

- Jargon, unfamiliar words, and inconsistent use of terms

- Inconsistent style and presentation of procedures

- Lack of consistency in capitalization and punctuation

- Lack of consistency in help window size and placement on screen

- Excessive or inconsistent indentation

- Tables and illustrations that require sideways scrolling to see

Causes

Inexperienced writers

In addition to the many possible writing problems mentioned earlier in this chapter, inexperienced writers may not follow the principles of good technical writing, including task orientation, information chunking, use of active voice, and so on. Appendix C, "For More Information," includes several good books on this topic.

Converting from another format

Many formatting problems arise when converting files from Microsoft Word or other programs into help files, particularly when styles have been used inconsistently or incorrectly.

Single-sourcing

Help material single-sourced from printed materials often needs modification to fit a screen format, but this often isn't done (usually because of lack of time).

Inadequate testing

Help is not checked online, so problems that don't show up in print aren't noticed.

Inadequate specifications and project style guide

Writers followed the specifications and style guide, but those documents weren't detailed enough. This is a particular problem on a project with several writers, or unskilled or inexperienced writers.

Browser problems

With browser-based help, some features may not work in all browsers, and different screen sizes and resolutions may change the appearance of the help in ways that cause problems.

Diagnosing the problem

- View the help online. Look for formatting problems, especially in tables and lists.

- Thoroughly copyedit the file, looking at format and presentation as well as content.

- If the help is browser-based, check it at different resolutions, screen sizes, and font sizes.

Cures

- As needed, rewrite, change paragraph styles, and make other formatting changes.

- Consider some tables and figures. Are they needed? If so, can they be changed to better fit an online format?

- Revise the specifications.

See Chapter 10, "Copyediting and Production Editing," for details.

Table 1. To diagnose and cure common help problems, do these things before shipping the help. Better still, plan and write the help so these problems do not occur.

Do this...	Ask these questions...	To diagnose this problem	Cure for the problem	More info here
Using sample questions, test index	Can I find the answer to the questions using the index?	Poor indexing	Edit index; add, delete, or reword entries	Chapter 6
Using sample questions, test table of contents (ToC)	Can I find the answer to the questions using the ToC?	Poor ToC organization	Edit ToC; reorganize order of topics	Chapter 6
		Poor topic titles	Reword topic titles	Chapter 10
If you can't find the information using index or ToC, search the help	Is the information in the help file?	Missing information, poor index	Write new topics or improve index	Chapter 6
Select random topics in help	Do topics have links to related topics, for a bigger picture?	Poor internal linking	Add or reword links	Chapter 10
	Do topics make sense out of context?	Unclear or incomplete topics	Add brief explanations	
	Does help open at dialog-level or procedural topics?	Help always opens at ToC or index	Programming change	
	Are topics long, requiring lots of scrolling? Are paragraphs of explanation mixed with procedures? Do topics contain several overlapping ideas, or if–then branching?	Too much detail	Split into several linked topics Use pop-ups for brief explanationsCut out unnecessary information	Chapter 8
	Do topics (particularly for fields and controls) say only the obvious?	Not enough detail	Add information or relevant links to existing information	Chapter 8

Table 1, continued

Do this...	Ask these questions...	To diagnose this problem	Cure for the problem	More info here
Attempt to complete sample tasks	Can I find necessary information in the help topic associated with the dialogs used in the task? Is help available for controls as well as dialogs? Do procedural topics provide context, or include links to more information?	Missing information, poor linking	Add information or relevant links to existing information	
Check for similar dialogs that share one help topic	Does the help information make sense for each dialog? Is the help topic too long and complex, or too general?	Too much or not enough detail	Programming change Revise help to cover all situations Break into several topics, if necessary	Chapter 8
Check help against specifications and style guide	Do the various topic types follow the specifications?	Inconsistency or poor writing	Revise content of topics	
	Does help follow specifications, but still have problems?	Inadequate specifications or style guide	Revise specifications	Appendix A
	Is the help topic trying to cover several variations of a dialog?	Programming problem (for example, two dialogs calling same help topic)	Negotiate change in program or links to help	
Check help against developed product	Does product work the way the help says it does?	Incomplete or incorrect information in help	Rewrite help topic or link to other information	Chapter 8
	Are any dialogs without help?	Missing information	Write new topic	
	Are any fields or controls not mentioned anywhere in help?	Missing information	Add information to existing topic, or write new topic	
Check compiled help on different monitors or resolutions	Does help display correctly? Check tables and illustrations, and numbered and bulleted lists.	Display problems	Rewrite or reformat	Chapter 10
Bring in novice users to test the help	Can they find answers to their questions using the help?	Most problems	Look in relevant chapter of this book for suggestions	

Categorizing problem severity

When you don't have time to fix all the problems, use the principles of triage to categorize the severity of problems. Make sure that category 1 problems are fixed before the help ships (or alert the product manager of possible serious consequences). Fix as many category 2 problems as you can in the time available. You might want to subdivide this group by severity (fix the worst) or by time required to fix them (fix lots of easy ones). If necessary, leave category 3 problems until the next release.

- Category 1: Errors that must be fixed because the content is factually incorrect or the wording is unclear or ambiguous and may lead to serious misunderstanding; or changes that are required for legal reasons.

- Category 2: Changes that improve the writing or presentation but are not essential to understanding.

- Category 3: Changes that others might consider pedantic nitpicking, and that the vast majority of the audience won't care about or probably even notice. (Many grammatical and usage errors are in this category.)

Conclusion

Use the hints provided in this chapter to plan and write online help so it avoids users' most common complaints. Prioritize problems and fix the most serious first.

Updates and corrections to this chapter can be found on Hentzenwerke's Web site, **www.hentzenwerke.com**. Click "Catalog" and navigate to the page for this book.

Chapter 6
Producing the Table of Contents and Index

Readers use the table of contents or the index to look up information not immediately associated with the visible window or dialog box, when they want answers to "can I?" or "how do I?" or "where is?" questions. This chapter describes ways to make the table of contents and index useful from the readers' point of view, so they can find information quickly and easily.

Readers use a help system's table of contents or index in several situations:

- When the help system always opens at the table of contents, and does not have a relevant help topic linked to each application dialog, window, or page.

- When they want to look up information not associated with the application window that is currently open.

- When the help system opens to a "What do you want help with?" dialog that provides sample choices and a text-entry box, if they find the choices irrelevant to their question.

A well-designed table of contents and index will help many readers locate the information they require. If their first few attempts at using these retrieval aids don't help, readers will often reject the help as useless and not look at it again.

Of course, a great table of contents and index are not enough—you also need to make sure that the topics contain the necessary information.

 If users can't find the information they want in the help, for all practical purposes the information is not there, no matter how well it's written.

Terminology

Table of contents

A *table of contents* provides readers with a hierarchical view of the topic titles in your help system. When readers select a topic listed in the table of contents, they are taken directly to that topic. You can organize the table of contents by subject or by category, and you can include a topic under more than one heading (unlike in a printed book), so readers have more than one way to find it. (Programmers often call this an "index.")

Index

An *index* contains keywords that the writer specifies. It can therefore contain terms for beginners and advanced users, synonyms for terms, terms that describe topics generally, and terms that describe topics specifically. A well-developed index can provide readers with many different ways to find topics, in contrast to a table of contents which usually provides only one way to find each topic.

Search

Some readers prefer to use the *Search* function instead of the index. Using Search, they can locate every topic that contains a particular word or phrase. This technique may assist them in locating poorly indexed topics, but may also give them a long list of irrelevant topics to wade through. Search is also limited to words that actually appear in the help topics, and thus does not find synonyms.

Designing a useful table of contents

A draft table of contents should have emerged from the audience analysis, task analysis, outlining, mapping, and prototyping steps of your help project, or you may have deliberately prepared one during the planning process. If you don't already have a draft table of contents, create one during the writing stage.

Topic titles and the structure of the table of contents need to be logical from the readers' point of view, which may be quite different from the developers' point of view. For example, developers might group topics by program functions, which do not always correspond with users' tasks—but users are far more likely to want to know how to *do* something.

Structure

The structure of a table of contents for online help should be similar to the structure of a table of contents in a printed book, but the best sequence of topics for a help system may be different from the best sequence for a printed book. You might begin with tasks usually done first and progress in a chronological order, or begin with common tasks and progress to less-common ones, or begin with easy tasks and progress to more difficult or complicated ones. Many help systems group topics into Getting Started, Procedures (or How To), and Reference, or other logical groupings for different needs and skill levels.

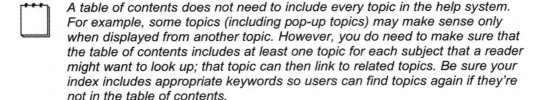

A table of contents does not need to include every topic in the help system. For example, some topics (including pop-up topics) may make sense only when displayed from another topic. However, you do need to make sure that the table of contents includes at least one topic for each subject that a reader might want to look up; that topic can then link to related topics. Be sure your index includes appropriate keywords so users can find topics again if they're not in the table of contents.

Presentation

The table of contents can be presented in various ways, but the basic structure is the same in each case. The presentation you choose may depend on the type of help you're producing (WinHelp, Microsoft HTML Help, HTML-based help, or some other form), the capabilities of the help-authoring software you're using, and your users' expectations and preferences.

Expanding tree structure

You can organize topics using icons to identify main topics and subtopics. For example, in Microsoft HTML Help, if you use the default icons, book icons represent groups of topics and page icons represent individual topics, as illustrated in Figure 2). Users can double-click a book icon to expand it to show other book or page icons. You can change the default icons or create your own icons. Variations are to use ⊞ and ⊟ icons, or a combination of book and page icons and ⊞ and ⊟ icons, as shown in Figure 6).

A page of ordinary links

You may prefer to provide the table of contents as a page of ordinary links, as in a printed book. This technique is useful when users are unable or unlikely to have the table of contents visible while reading specific topics (as on a Web site). It's also useful in an extensive help system, if you don't want to put too many levels of the hierarchy into the main table of contents. Users can pick a topic from the main list and be presented with a more detailed page. Figure 8 shows an example of a table of contents that uses ordinary links.

Reviewing a table of contents

During the writing and editing steps, you need to review the table of contents to see if it's suitable for your audience. Many problems are not obvious from a cursory look; you need to ask a lot of questions *from the users' point of view* before you discover some problems.

1. Look at the structure of the table of contents. Does it make sense to you? Ask others what they think. Involve real users, if possible.

2. Make some sample questions from your task list and try to find the answers to those questions, using the table of contents.

Table 1 is a checklist of general questions to ask when reviewing a table of contents, and also explains how to fix common problems.

Table 1. *Checklist of questions to ask when reviewing a table of contents.*

Problem	Solution
Is the flow of information logical from the readers' point of view?	Rearrange the sequence of headings and topics.
Are the topic titles (headings) informative? Are they task-oriented?	Reword as necessary.
Is information missing?	Add some headings (and possibly some topics to go with them).
Is the table of contents too detailed (contains too many heading levels) or not detailed enough (contains too few heading levels)?	Add or delete some headings or subheadings. Rearrange the sequence of headings and topics.
Are the headings too long or too short? Are they parallel in structure? Is the presentation consistent?	Copyedit.
Do any entries jump to the wrong topic?	Change entry to point to the correct topic.

Example 1. Table of contents with subtle problems

The table of contents shown in **Figure 1** (from Eudora Pro, a popular e-mail program) looks reasonably good at this level, but when you expand some headings and start asking questions, you may find some important concepts missing from the place you expect to find them.

Figure 1. *A table of contents with one heading expanded to show another level.*

In **Figure 2**, the "Get Started" heading has been expanded. Nowhere could I find an overview of the product or the parts of the window I am likely to see when I first open the product.

Eudora Pro has some "What's this?" help in the interface, but most parts of the main window display the unhelpful message "No help topic is associated with this item." Nor is the information in the *User Guide* (supplied as a PDF); its contents are almost identical to those in the online help, with the addition of some screen shots.

If I expanded some other headings and looked for logical places to find answers to my questions, I found that many other bits of information were missing. Some of this information was in fact buried in the help somewhere, but I couldn't find it using the table of contents.

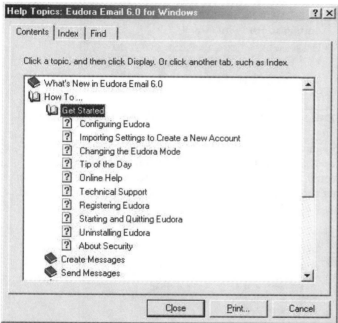

Figure 2. A subheading has been expanded to show individual topics.

Example 2. A more user-friendly table of contents

Figure 3 is taken from another e-mail program, Microsoft Outlook Express, which uses HTML Help. It displays the table of contents on the left and the selected topic on the right.

The "Getting started" section is a single page containing introductory information (not shown here) and links to more information, instead of a heading (book icon) with associated pages in the contents list. This technique works well in this type of display, and puts the various topics into perspective.

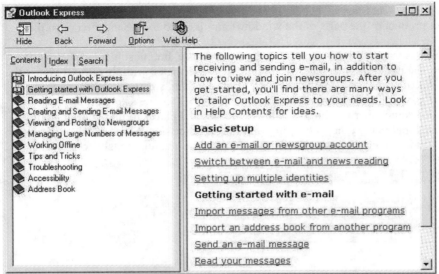

Figure 3. *Table of contents showing a different approach to Getting Started topics.*

Figure 4 shows the same table of contents with the next heading, "Reading Mail Messages," expanded. The first topic under this heading is "Read your messages," which takes you to the same topic you would find if you had selected the "Read your messages" link in the "Getting started" topic. This sort of repetition can be extremely helpful to users, who may approach a question from many different angles.

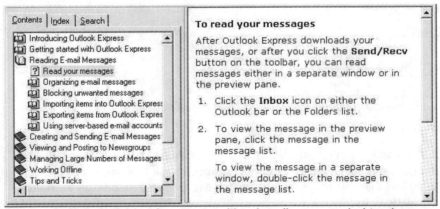

Figure 4. *Sample table of contents with a heading expanded to show pages (topics). Notice the different icons for "how to" topics ([?]) and conceptual topics ([□]).*

Example 3. Another user-friendly table of contents

The table of contents shown in this example is taken from the online help for Microsoft HTML Help Workshop.

Figure 5 shows the fully collapsed table of contents on the left. The reader can tell that several different types of information are included, grouped in logical ways. The first topic (shown on the right) introduces the reader to the program.

Figure 6 shows the "Designing a Help System" heading and one of the subheadings expanded. The first topic in this section briefly summarizes what this section covers and provides links to conceptual and procedural topics.

Figure 5. Fully collapsed table of contents for a help system.

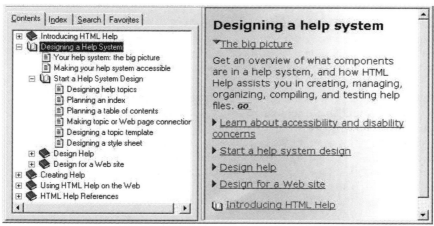

Figure 6. Table of contents with two headings expanded.

In **Figure 7**, the "Creating Help" heading has been expanded, along with one of its subheadings. The topics appear to be logically arranged and complete, so this table of contents shows no major structural problems. Whether the topics themselves have the information you want is another question.

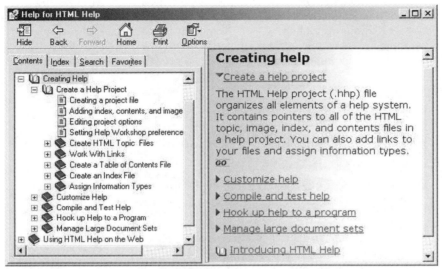

Figure 7. *Table of contents with several headings expanded.*

Example 4. A different approach: table of contents for a Web site

Web sites and Web applications vary greatly in the type of help provided. The help for some sites doesn't have anything resembling a table of contents, even when users might reasonably be expected to ask "What can I do on this site?" or "How do I do X?" Other sites offer a variety of ways to find information.

Figure 8 shows part of the first help page for the popular auction site, eBay (**http://www.ebay.com**). Notice that it includes a search box and links to an index and other sources of information.

The "Top Questions" topics listed in the central box vary depending on whether the user was signed in to eBay at the time, and what Web page was displayed when help was requested. Below the "Top Questions" is a collection of links arranged in a manner similar to the browse lists on many Web sites.

The overall result is that users have numerous ways to find information by using familiar techniques.

Figure 8. Contents page for eBay Web site, March 2004.

Designing a useful index

You need to put as much, or more, care into creating an index for online help as you would put into creating an index for printed documentation. Use the same general principles for creating index entries (called *keywords* in most help-authoring systems) for online help as for printed documents.

A full treatment of indexing, and the selection of appropriate keywords, is beyond the scope of this book. Look in Appendix C, "For More Information," for some suggested books on indexing. Chapter 9, "Creating the index," in Boggan *et al.* (*Developing Online Help for Windows 95*, 1999) is particularly good.

 Most help-authoring tools provide ways to assist you in creating new entries and editing the resulting index. Most tools can also create index entries automatically from topic titles, but these entries require a lot of editing. Although some of the automatically generated index entries will be useful, many others will be noise, and many valuable index entries (such as second-level entries) won't be created at all. Examine the index closely to identify and fix these problems.

If you are creating an HTML-based help system using software that does not provide a built-in indexing function, you might consider using a tool such as HTML Indexer; for more information, see Appendix B, "Help Types and Tools."

Reviewing an index

When reviewing an index, follow these steps:

1. Take some sample questions from your task list and try to find the answers, using the index.

2. Do some random lookups in the help, to see whether the term or topic is in the index. If several random selections are not in the index, you may need to do more work to make the index useful.

Table 2 shows a checklist of questions to ask when reviewing an index, and also explains how to fix common problems.

Table 2. Checklist of questions to ask when reviewing an index.

Problem	Solution
Is the first word of each index entry meaningful (something the reader is likely to be looking for)?	Reword.
Does a main entry for the name of the product have numerous subentries under it?	Turn the subentries into main entries.
Do insignificant differences in capitalization or plurals cause separate index entries to appear, rather than one entry with more than one subentry? (This often occurs when two or more help files are combined, or when more than one writer is involved in indexing.)	Either make the entries into subentries of one keyword, or delete some of them.
Do duplicate main entries occur, with no indication of the difference between them?	Either make the entries into subentries of one keyword, or make the difference explicit in the main entries.
Do some entries contain too little detail? For example, a keyword may refer to a control but give no indication of context.	Add a word or two to the index entry to make it more meaningful, or delete the entry.
Do some entries have too much detail? For example, a main entry may have several subentries, but all the subentries point to the same topic.	Change the subentries into main entries, retaining the original main entry but removing the subentries beneath it.
Do all topics have a main entry, not just a subentry? (They might also have a subentry.)	Add main entries as needed. These entries should be keywords, not the topic title (unless the two are the same).
Do any "see" references point to an entry that does not have subentries? For example, if your index includes "Search, see Find" but "Find" has no subentries, it refers to only one topic.	Remove the "see" reference and point the entry directly to a topic. In this example, both "Search" and "Find" would point to the same topic.
Are any entries or subentries irrelevant? (This often happens when reusing material written for another purpose or another product.)	Remove the irrelevant entries and subentries from the keyword list.
Do any main entries have only one subentry?	Combine the subentry into the main entry.
Do all keywords jump to the correct topics?	Change as needed.

Problem	Solution
Are any concepts and synonyms (from the list you prepared earlier) missing from the index? Some things to check for: • Non-technical terms for beginning users • Technical terms for advanced users • Common synonyms for technical terms • Words that describe the topic generally • Words that describe part of the topic • Inverted forms—for example, "adding a signature" and "signature, adding" • Words or phrases that appear in tool tips, menu items, dialog boxes, and context-sensitive help topics	Add those concepts and synonyms as keywords, pointing to appropriate topics.

Example 5. An index with problems

Figure 9 is taken from Eudora Pro 4.2. You can see some index entries that might need some work. For example, "Adding" is a separate entry, and there are four other "Adding ..." entries, one of which looks a bit suspicious—"Adding: Moving, and Removing Toolbar Buttons."

You can guess that some of the entries—for example, "Add (Checking Spelling dialog)— are for controls such as menu-bar or toolbar items. However, you can't be sure about some of the others.

I guessed that "Add as Recipient" is another control (it is), and that "Adding" would either take me to a general discussion about adding something, or it would display a list of help topics about adding specific things. In fact, "Adding" opened the same help topic as "Adding: Moving, and Removing Toolbar Buttons" because the index keyword was incorrectly coded.

All the guesses I made about the "Address Book" entry were wrong. If you choose that, you get a "Topics Found" dialog with two choices, "Address Book" (which opens an out-of-context field-help topic) and "Address Book (Product-HLP)" which opens a long topic describing an address book and how to use it.

If you select index entries at random, you'll find that a pattern almost emerges: Most of the keywords starting with "-ing" words (for example, Adding, Sending, Linking) lead to how-to or procedural topics, and any keyword containing a dialog name in parentheses, such as "Add (Checking Spelling dialog)" leads to a short (pop-up style) description of a field or menu item. Unfortunately, you'll also find that many keywords don't fit either pattern, and many of them lead to field-help topics with no indication of where the control is located.

Pop-up topics, particularly for fields and controls, usually should not be indexed—but if you do index them, make sure to put some context information in the index entry, and preferably include a link to the topic with which the pop-up is associated. If you think that users will look for the function or concept given in the pop-up topic, consider pointing that index entry to the topic from which the pop-up is linked, rather than to the pop-up topic itself.

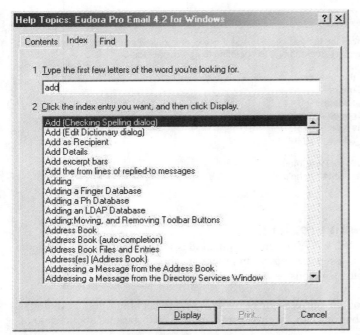

Figure 9. Sample help index with problems.

Example 6. A better index for an e-mail program

Figure 10 shows the same index from Version 6.0 of Eudora Pro. As you can see, the index has been improved. The inappropriate "Add[ing]" entries are no longer there, and the field help entries now clearly show the dialog with which they are associated.

Example 7. An index with clearly differentiated entries

Figure 11 and **Figure 12** are samples of the index from Microsoft Outlook Express. The index appears on the left and the selected topic on the right.

This help system shows a long list of "adding" keywords; each has enough information for the reader to tell what the topic is about.

Further investigation, as shown in Figure 12, reveals that you can find the same topic by searching for the inverted keyword ("signature"), as you should be able to do.

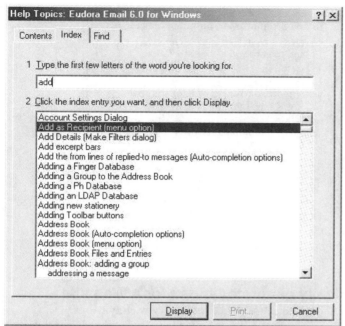

Figure 10. Improved help index for an e-mail program.

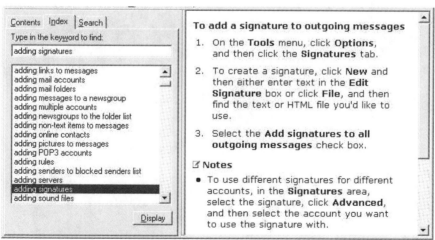

Figure 11. Example of an index with clearly differentiated keywords.

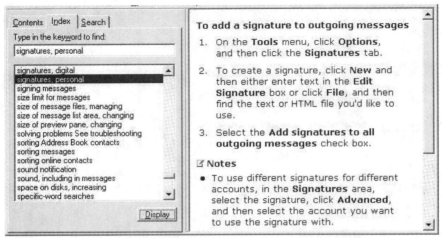

Figure 12. Example of inverted keyword that leads to the same topic.

Example 8. An automatically generated index for a Web site

Figure 13 shows part of the index for the eBay Web site, **http://www.ebay.com**.

The eBay help index is simply an alphabetic listing of the help topic titles. In most cases, the topic titles are informative, so perhaps this index is sufficient to meet the needs of users of this site. However, in general I consider this type of index to be inadequate, as it contains no synonyms or keywords not used in the topic titles.

Figure 13. Index for help system on eBay Web site, March 2004.

Example 9. A bad example: combining index and search

Starting with Microsoft Office 2000, the help combines the index and the Search function into a single "Index" option, making it less useful for both purposes.

When readers enter index or search terms, they are presented with a list of topics (see **Figure 14**), many of which often turn out to be irrelevant. Although the first few topics on the list have a good chance of answering the reader's question, quite often they don't. The reader is left with the choice of either wading through the long list of topics hoping to stumble on the answer to the real question, or giving up in despair. Most readers give up.

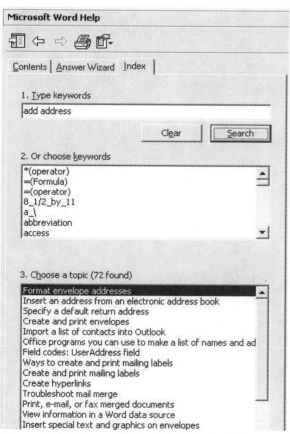

Figure 14. Microsoft Word 2000 help index, combined with Search. The list of topics retrieved is several times as long as the portion shown here.

Conclusion

Tables of contents and indexes are important retrieval aids for users, but to be useful they must be carefully designed to meet those users' needs and not contain irrelevant, confusing, or misleading entries. Good retrieval aids are very important in encouraging readers to use the help. If they can't quickly find the topic they want, readers often won't look at the help again.

Updates and corrections to this chapter can be found on Hentzenwerke's Web site, **www.hentzenwerke.com**. Click "Catalog" and navigate to the page for this book.

Chapter 7
Providing Navigation
and Context

Navigation includes all the ways for readers to move around in a help system and find the information they want. Context helps readers keep track of where they are, how they got there, and what happens next. This chapter describes some methods for providing navigation and context.

Good *navigation* methods ensure that users have clearly defined paths from where they are in the help system to any other information they may need at that point.

Navigation within a help system includes:

- Providing a table of contents, index, and search function (discussed in Chapter 6, "Producing the Table of Contents and Index")

- Using cross-references and other links

- Using expanding sections

- Providing for reader-defined navigation

- Using visual aids such as icons or color

- Using browse sequences (Next and Previous)

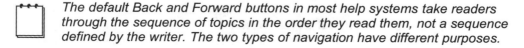 *The default Back and Forward buttons in most help systems take readers through the sequence of topics in the order they read them, not a sequence defined by the writer. The two types of navigation have different purposes.*

Context covers such questions as "Where am I?", "How did I get here?", "What larger task does this little piece fit into?", and "What happens next?" Context is particularly relevant to readers who found a topic from the index or table of contents, and is very important when those are the only ways to access the help topics. Here are some ways to provide context:

- Show the path to a topic.

- Provide context information in the text.

- Tell users what to expect, and where to find troubleshooting help if something unexpected happens.

Avoiding problems

A good time to diagnose and avoid many potential problems is at the detailed prototype stage. (See "Building a detailed contents prototype" in Chapter 4, "Prototyping the Help System.") Later, as you begin writing the help topics, check a sample for symptoms of navigation and context problems. Refine your writing based on the results of the sample.

When evaluating the prototype help, ask these questions about each topic:

- Does the topic contain all the information you need at that point? (Sometimes topics contain *too much* information, a problem that we'll look at in Chapter 8, "Meeting the Needs of Novices to Experts.")

- If the topic does not contain all the information you need, does it include links to other topics that fill in the gaps?

- Can you tell how this topic fits in with what you want to do? Does it matter? (In some cases, it doesn't matter; in other cases, it matters very much.)

- If a topic tells you how to do something, do you know where to find that function in the application?

- Does the topic tell you about anything you need to do first, before you do this step?

Ideally, during a review you will evaluate every topic for navigation and context, but in practice you can usually make a good judgment of overall problems by checking a sample.

If some of your help topics fail any of these tests, use the ideas in the rest of this chapter to help you decide how to write the help system correctly.

 Minor changes in a help system can often make a major improvement in usability.

Using cross-references and other links

You can provide jumps or links within a help file or to resources outside a help system. The most common links are those within a help file, from one help file to another, or from a help file to a Web site or server location. Linked files can include video, audio, and graphics (animated or static) as well as text.

Cross-references and other links can take several forms, all based on the same technology. **Figure 1** shows examples of three types of links:

- Links to other topics, files, or locations from within the text of the topic

- Links to pop-up topics, including glossary topics

- Links collected in a "related topics" or "see also" section of the topic

See "Help navigation scheme" in Chapter 3, "Developing Specifications," for information on planning a consistent set of cross-references and other links.

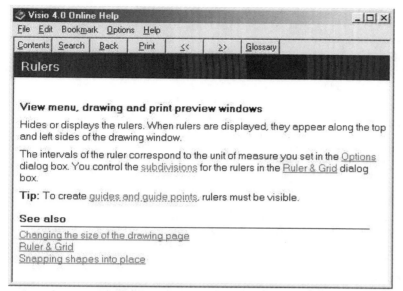

Figure 1. *A help topic containing text links to pop-up topics (dotted underlines), other topics (solid underlines), and "see also" references.*

Links to other topics, files, or locations

You can create a text link to jump from one topic to another within a help project, or from a help topic to another help file or an external Web site or other location. A text link usually consists of a word or a short phrase (see Figure 1). Some links may be from graphics such as icons, instead of from text. The graphic may be associated with some explanatory text.

 It's just as bad to have too many links as it is to have too few links, if they distract or confuse readers. You want to provide easy ways to find information, but you don't want to overwhelm readers with side issues or other details.

Links to pop-up topics, including glossary topics

You can create a text link to open a pop-up topic (see **Figure 2**) or in some cases display glossary information as a "mouseover" (text that appears when users rest a mouse pointer on a link). Pop-ups and mouseovers differ mainly in the techniques used to produce them. As with other links, be careful not to include too many.

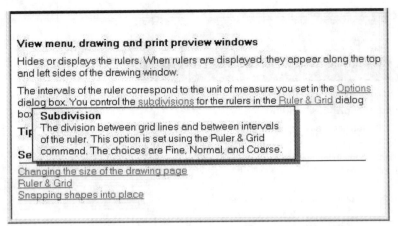

Figure 2. The help topic shown in Figure 1, with one of the pop-up topics displayed.

Related topic references

Related topics can be provided in various ways, including text links collected at the end of a help topic (under a heading such as "See also," "For more information," or "Related topics") or as a dialog box or pop-up menu (reached from a Related Topics button). However they are presented, the purpose is the same: to provide links to related information and assist in keeping topics short and to the point by not including everything the reader might want to know about a subject in one long, scrolling topic.

For example, a procedural topic might be related to a conceptual topic, one or more general help topics for the dialog boxes mentioned in the procedure, and a frequently-asked-questions topic.

Figure 1 shows related topics displayed as a list within the original help topic. **Figure 3** shows a different way to provide related topics: a clickable link which pops up a list of topics.

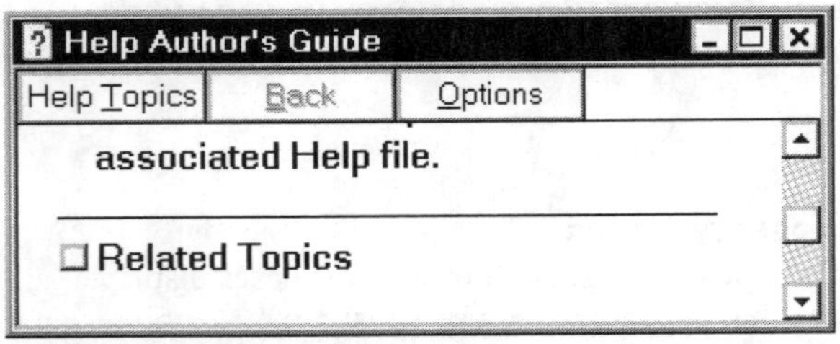

Figure 3. This Related Topics link pops up a list of topics.

Some topics do not require a Related Topics section; don't include one if it isn't necessary. Do not include related topics in pop-up field-level help topics that are accessed from dialog-level topics or *What's this?* help. Links from within pop-up topics often don't work; when they do, the Back function often won't take the reader back to the pop-up topic.

You can provide Related Topics links as short phrases or include one-sentence descriptions. Links with descriptions are often presented in a "definition list" format, which is recommended for Web pages but can be useful in many other situations as well. Compare these lists of links:

Example of a link list without descriptions
See also:
Chapter 6
Chapter 8
Chapter 9

Example of a link list with brief descriptions
See also:
Chapter 6, Producing the Table of Contents and Index
Chapter 8, Meeting the Needs of Novices to Experts
Chapter 9, Linking from Application to Help

Example of links with longer descriptions presented as a definition list
See also:
Chapter 6, Producing the Table of Contents and Index
> Diagnosing problems, what to look for, how to fix problems, and examples of good and bad tables of contents and indexes.

Chapter 8, Meeting the Needs of Novices to Experts
> Some common problems, with suggestions for how to overcome them; also, how to try to provide information for everyone, at the right level of detail.

Chapter 9, Linking from Application to Help
> How to avoid linking problems by agreeing with programmers on how linking will be done, and some suggestions for overcoming problems if these agreements are not followed.

Reviewing cross-references and other links

Here are some things to look for when reviewing cross-references and other links. Many of these issues could be dealt with at the planning stage by creating a table of topics and links; for an example, see Figure 3 in Chapter 2, "Analyzing Audiences and Tasks."

- First revisit the help specifications, to remind yourself of the types of help topics that were supposed to have links to other types of help topics. Does each topic include the specified links?

- Do cross-reference links within the text distract or confuse the reader? If the referenced material is not essential to the flow of information, it's often better to put the links in a separate paragraph, or group them at the end of the topic. Many people will try to look at every link provided, afraid they might miss something important.

- Do text links lead to unnecessary glossary and other small pop-up windows? Include glossary links if they serve a useful purpose, but be selective in choosing which terms have links to explanatory material. Too many pop-ups can be distracting.

- Pay particular attention to the wording of links, which are often derived from topic titles and may not contain enough information to let readers know if what's at the other end of the link is what they're looking for.

- Are text links self-explanatory? Do readers get a good idea of what they will find if they click on the link? If not, can you reword the link, or add a short description (phrase or sentence) to each link?

Using expanding sections

You can use expanding sections in a help topic to hide or show details within a help topic itself, instead of using pop-up topics or jumping to separate topics. This technique has the advantage that readers can print the topic with some or all of the details showing, if they wish. **Figure 4** shows a topic with one section expanded. Compare this figure with Figure 7 in Chapter 6, "Producing the Table of Contents and Index," which shows the first link expanded.

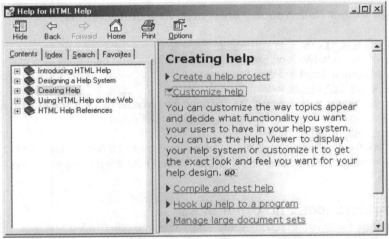

Figure 4. When these links (marked by small arrows) are clicked, extra information is displayed below the link. Clicking the link again hides the extra information.

Providing for reader-defined navigation

Help systems can provide several ways for readers to specify some navigation features they find useful. These features include:

- Navigation pane
- Bookmarks and Favorites
- History list

Navigation pane

The default HTML Help window has a navigation pane on the left. The navigation pane usually includes tabs for Contents, Index, and Search, but writers can change these tabs. **Figure 5** shows a Favorites tab in the navigation pane.

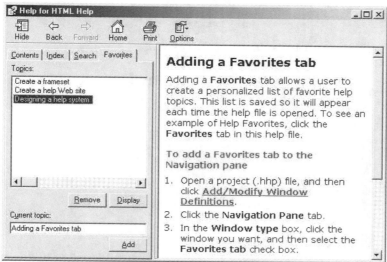

Figure 5. The Favorites tab in the Navigation pane of HTML Help.

Writers can design compiled help files so that the navigation pane is automatically hidden when a reader clicks outside of the HTML Help Viewer. This allows the reader to see more of the screen when working in a software program. When the reader clicks inside the help topic, the navigation pane is reopened.

Help-authoring tools can place the navigation pane in other locations (for example, to the right of the help topic), and can provide a similar function in help for Web pages.

Bookmarks and Favorites

Using Bookmarks or Favorites, readers can build a list of the help topics they often use. You should make sure those features are enabled in the help files you create. (Web browsers usually have one of these features available as a standard feature.)

Figure 5 shows a Favorites tab in the navigation pane of HTML Help. **Figure 6** shows a Bookmark item on a WinHelp menu bar. **Figure 7** shows Bookmarks items in two places on each of two Web browsers, Opera and Microsoft Internet Explorer.

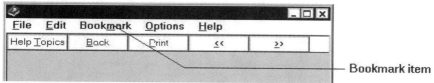

Figure 6. A Bookmark item on the menu bar of a primary help window.

History list (Web browsers)

Many users find a history list useful when they think, "I looked at X yesterday; I wonder where I found it?" Web browsers provide history lists (see Figure 7 for examples); some help-authoring tools may allow writers to specify history lists in other forms of online help.

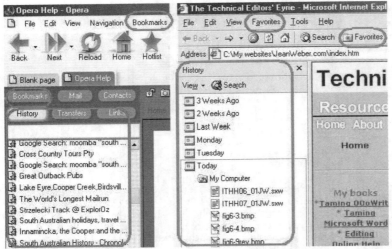

Figure 7. Examples of Bookmarks and Favorites menu bar items and toolbar buttons, as well as a history list, in the Web browsers Opera and Internet Explorer.

Using visual aids such as icons or color

Writers can use icons, color, and other visual aids to help readers orient themselves and navigate through the help file. For example, icons might distinguish:

- Different information types, such as conceptual help, procedural help, dialog-level help, and frequently-asked-questions help

- Different expertise levels, such as beginner, intermediate, and advanced

- Mandatory processes, steps, or fields; tips; optional processes; and warnings

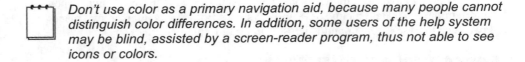

Don't use color as a primary navigation aid, because many people cannot distinguish color differences. In addition, some users of the help system may be blind, assisted by a screen-reader program, thus not able to see icons or colors.

Reviewing visual aids

Some questions to ask:

- If visual aids are used in the help file, are they helpful or are they confusing or irrelevant?

- Are navigational icons or colors used consistently? That is, do similar topics have the same icons, used in the same way, placed in the same spot in the topic?

- Is color a primary navigation aid? If so, reconsider your design.

- Is the meaning of the icons clear to the reader, or is some quick and easy way provided for the reader to find out what the icon means?

 Keep it simple! Many people won't notice your cleverly designed color coding or cute icons, or they won't realize they have any significance—even if you provide an explanation somewhere in the help file.

Using browse sequences

A browse sequence is the order in which writers link a series of topics together so readers can move easily from one topic to the next or previous topic in the sequence.

Writers can define more than one browse sequence for a help file, but any one topic can appear in only one browse sequence. Readers cannot move from one browse sequence to another by using the browse buttons.

Using a single browse sequence

For a book-like file, such as an online user guide, the browse sequence could be the same as the order of topics in the contents list. Readers can then move through the sequence of topics much like turning the pages of a book, or they can use the hypertext links to jump from one spot to another, or use any combination of browsing and jumping.

Using more than one browse sequence

Writers might decide to define more than one browse sequence. For example, they could:

- Put a series of procedural topics in one sequence, with reference topics in another sequence and conceptual topics in a third.

- Set up browse sequences for novice and advanced users.

In these cases, depending on where readers jump into the help file, they can browse easily through one type of material without being distracted by another type of material. (Advanced users in particular appreciate being able to avoid reading tutorial material appropriate for novices.) Writers can also provide hypertext links between browse sequences.

Are browse sequences useful? Do readers use them?

Answers to these questions may come from your audience analysis. Probably some readers find browse sequences useful, in some circumstances. For example, if a help file (or a portion of it) is presented as an online book, or if a topic clearly indicates that it is continued in another topic (as shown in **Figure 8**), readers are more likely to use a browse sequence than if they are seeking a quick, memory-jogging piece of help or a short how-to procedure.

WinHelp

In WinHelp, readers move forward or backward through the defined sequence of topics by using the Browse buttons (<< and >>) on the Help window (see Figure 8). If a topic does not belong to a browse sequence, the browse buttons are disabled (that is, they are visible but are grayed out and do not work). Writers can also define the help file to not display browse buttons if they choose not to provide any browse sequences.

Many users do not understand the function of browse buttons and sequences, and may become frustrated if some topics are in a sequence and others are not. Writers might assist such users by providing other clues within the help text. Figure 8 shows an interesting example of a WinHelp topic that provides browse buttons as well as Back and Next buttons to encourage readers to step through the eight topics on this subject. The topic title clearly shows that the subject contains more than one help topic, a valuable cue for readers when Back and Next buttons are not used.

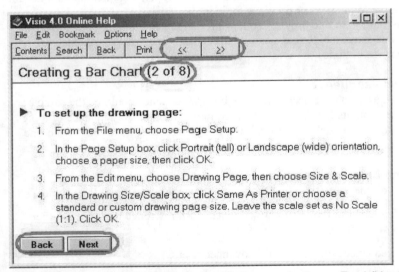

Figure 8. Example of a help topic with browse buttons, Back/Next buttons, and a clear indication that this topic is one of a series.

HTML Help
In HTML Help, writers can provide browse sequences by adding Next and Previous links to a series of Help topics, as shown in **Figure 9**. You could use a similar technique to put a browse sequence into HTML-based help on a Web site. Recent releases of some major help-authoring tools provide extra functions for creating browse sequences; check your tool's documentation for details.

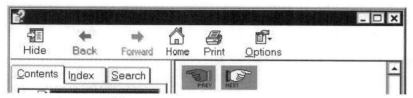

Figure 9. Top of HTML Help window, showing Previous and Next buttons inserted by the writer in the text area, as well as the standard Back and Forward buttons on the toolbar.

Reviewing browse sequences
If the help file has browse sequences, check every sequence. Ask these questions:

- What is the purpose of this browse sequence? (Refer to the help specifications, which should have defined all the sequences.)

- Is the order of topics logical? If not, determine a better order.

- Are irrelevant topics included in the browse sequence? If so, remove them from the sequence (not from the help file).

- If any topics have internal links to other topics, what happens if readers follow one of those links? Are readers likely to return to the main sequence? Can you easily ensure they do return? If the linked topic is reached from more than one topic, you may not be able do this easily, but if the linked topic is reached from only this one topic, you could put a link back to the main topic.

- Should linked topics be part of the sequence, to improve the chances that readers will see them? Sometimes this is a good strategy; sometimes it isn't.

The answers to these questions depend on subjective judgments. To improve consistency, try to develop a policy for the use of browse sequences, especially when more than one writer is involved.

Providing context information in the text

Readers often find that the piece of help they've accessed is out of context. That is, they're not sure where they are, how they got there, what larger task this one fits into, or what happens next.

Writers should make sure each help topic contains enough information for readers to understand the context. Clues to readers can include:

- Cross-references (see "Using cross-references and other links" earlier in this chapter)
- Using breadcrumbs: showing the path to a topic
- Using words to provide context
- Telling users what to expect

Using breadcrumbs: showing the path to a topic

An orienting technique frequently seen on Web pages is to include at the top of a page or topic the path to that topic, like this:

Creating graphics > Creating a bar chart > Setting up a drawing page

Paths provide valuable context information, and readers can more easily jump up one or more levels in a hierarchy of topics to get a bigger picture when they want it. (These paths are commonly called *breadcrumbs*, a term taken from the Hansel and Gretel folk tale.)

Using words to provide context

You can often provide context using only a few words to set the scene or tell readers how to get to the relevant window or dialog. For example, Visio Express gives the context in the first line of each topic that describes a dialog, as shown in **Figure 10**.

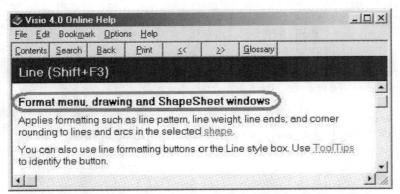

Figure 10. Example of a brief phrase providing context information. In this case, the phrase says where this command is active.

Telling users what to expect

Many users (particularly novices) are unsure what the results will be of a choice they make. Sometimes this is more a problem with the user interface itself, but often it occurs when users are not familiar with the terminology, or the program's behavior is different from other programs they may be used to.

Usually it's fairly easy to add a phrase or sentence to clarify what will happen when readers do something, and what to do if that doesn't happen. Provide a link to problem-solving or other topics; don't dump problem-solving information into a procedural topic.

Sometimes the best solution is to change the user interface, but if that isn't a choice, you need to make sure the help explains the situation clearly. Don't put in a lot of obvious information, but do keep in mind that if users can be confused by something, some of them definitely will be.

 Don't write long, involved explanations. If long explanations are necessary, put them in a separate topic and link to it.

Example 1. Which fields are required?

Problem. Filling in some fields on a dialog is required, but the dialog doesn't indicate which fields they are. If users leave some fields blank, they get an error message when they click OK. Even worse, the error message may not say which fields are required, leaving users to guess what they've done wrong.

In a related problem, neither the user interface nor the help tells users whether they can change the information they enter into required fields. Users wonder what happens if they make a mistake. Will they have to delete the record completely and re-enter it? Will it be in the database forever? Can they change it?

Solution. The user interface, the help, or both should tell users what the required fields are, whether users can leave some fields blank and fill them in later, or whether they can come back later and change information in the required fields.

Example 2. When is the data saved?

Problem. Some programs don't update the main database immediately when users save their data, but the user interface doesn't make this clear. Users may wonder where their data has gone and may even re-enter it.

Solution. The user interface, the help, or both should tell users how often the database is updated, if the update is not immediate.

Reviewing context information

Select topics at random. Ask the following questions:

- Do these topics make sense without prior knowledge of the product or process?

- Do the topics link to other topics, to give a bigger picture?

- Do the topics answer these questions, if the user interface doesn't answer them:

    - How did I get here (to this window, dialog, or page)?

    - Where do I go—or what do I do—next?

    - What does this control do, and should I be using it now? What is its purpose?

    - What happens if I choose this option instead of that one?

    - Will I be able to recover if my choice is not what I really wanted to do?

Conclusion

Good internal navigation, like good tables of contents and indexes, helps your readers find the information they need. Good context helps readers understand that information and use it to solve problems and complete tasks. This chapter described some ways to provide good navigation and context in your help systems.

Updates and corrections to this chapter can be found on Hentzenwerke's Web site, **www.hentzenwerke.com**. Click "Catalog" and navigate to the page for this book.

Chapter 8
Meeting the Needs of Novices to Experts

Readers often complain that the online help contains too little information; it gives only the obvious instructions or it describes the fields but gives no clue how to use them. Other readers complain that the help contains too much information; they can't find the answers to their questions in all the details. This chapter describes some common problems and suggests ways you can provide help that meets the needs of a range of users, at the right level of detail for each of them.

Quite often complaints of too much or too little information are made about the same help system, because the information is badly organized or presented. The challenge is to design a help system that meets the needs of a range of users, from novices to experts, without annoying any of them.

The best design depends on your users and their needs. What's best for an in-house system (linked perhaps to other information on an intranet) may not be the best—or even appropriate—for a product sold to people who may have a wide range of equipment and Internet connections.

The wrong level of detail often occurs because the writers had inadequate audience analysis information, were following inappropriate guidelines, or didn't take the time to think through the implications of what they included or excluded from the help.

Designing help to meet a range of users' needs

You should have some typical questions for each type or level of user. (Remember those personas and user/task matrixes described in Chapter 2, "Analyzing Audiences and Tasks"?) If you don't already have a list of typical questions, develop some now.

First, re-examine your specifications and audience analysis; consider the different user types you need to provide for, and their specific characteristics. See "Consider different user types" later in this chapter.

Next, consider these ideas and pick those that are suitable for your audience, or develop new ideas of your own:

- Divide information into topic or information types and aim some topics at different user types. See "Information types" later in this chapter.

- Include conceptual, overview, and advanced topics in the help system, not just procedural or field-level help. Use pop-ups for brief explanations. See "Content of topic types" in Chapter 3, "Developing Specifications," for more about these and other topic types.

- Link between different topic types and information levels. See "Using cross-references and other links" in Chapter 7, "Providing Navigation and Context."

- Cut out unnecessary details, digressions, and explanations.

- Describe alternative ways to use the application—for example, "If you aren't sure how the customer's name is spelled in the database, type the first three characters of the name and press F4. Scroll through the resulting list to find the required name."

- Use some form of embedded help for at least part of the explanatory information. See "Embedded help" later in this chapter.

- Provide wizards, coaches, show-me topics, or interactive tutorials to assist beginners. These features are often part of a performance support system, which can be integrated with online manuals or company documents. See "Assistance for novice users" later in this chapter.

- Use techniques for hiding or showing information, such as pop-ups, expanding hot spots, secondary windows, sidebars, and others.

- Provide a way for users to choose to keep help on top of the application or beside the application, or to hide the help.

- Provide a means for experts to skip simplified explanations and turn off reminders, wizards, and other forms of help. See "Providing for users' preferences" later in this chapter.

Consider different user types

JoAnn Hackos and Dawn Stevens (*Standards for Online Communication*, 1997, pages 31–46) discuss the characteristics, needs, and preferences of users in five "stages of use" (levels of knowledge and experience): Novice, Advanced Beginner, Competent Performer, Proficient Performer, and Expert Performer. They suggest some ways to support those needs and preferences.

Some of the characteristics include the following (all quotes from Hackos and Stevens):

- "Novices don't want to learn, only accomplish a goal."

- "Advanced beginners try tasks on their own ... have difficulty troubleshooting ... [and] want information fast."

- "Competent performers develop conceptual models ... troubleshoot problems on their own ... [and] seek out expert user advice."

- "Proficient performers want to understand the larger conceptual framework ... are frustrated by oversimplified information ... [and] learn from the experience of others."

- "Expert performers are primary sources of knowledge and information ... [and] continually look for better methods."

Many people prefer a scheme that divides the audience into three groups: novices, experts, and occasional users. (An occasional user is somewhat different from the others and has different needs in both the user interface and the Help system.)

Whatever scheme you use, your help system needs to cater to the ability levels and attitudes of users in all of these stages. You should address these issues during the planning stage of the project and include them in the specifications. See Table 1 in Chapter 3, "Developing Specifications."

 An individual might be an expert user of some parts of a program, an occasional user of other parts, and a complete novice in still other parts.

Define different information types

You can define whatever information types are appropriate for the project and audience. For example, you might define topics to correspond to user types (novice, intermediate, or expert) or you might define them by content (procedure, concept, reference, instruction). The HTML Help Workshop suggests other ideas: topics corresponding to components of the software, when users may purchase or install a subset of the components; topics for developers or system administrators, which ordinary users won't see; and topics corresponding to different operating systems.

You can group different information types or present them to users in different ways, including:

- Set up the help contents page to group information into types, as shown in **Figure 1**.

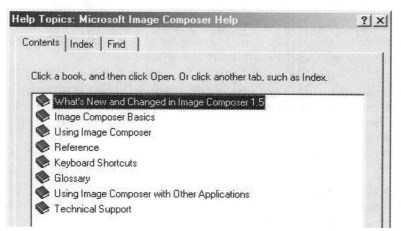

Figure 1. Example of a contents page grouped by information type.

- Put information categories on the Help menu, as shown in **Figure 2**. Link the Help menu items to topics containing tables of contents or other links to relevant information. (Adding items to a menu may require cooperation from the programmers.)

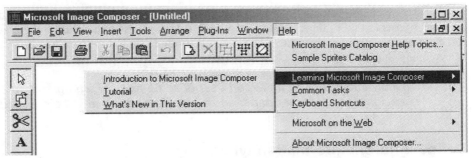

Figure 2. *Sample Help menu showing some information categories.*

- Provide browse sequences, icons, or other navigational aids to assist some users in finding appropriate information. For example, within a reference section, you could link all of the programming topics in alphabetical order in a browse sequence. See "Using browse sequences" in Chapter 7, "Providing Navigation and Context," for more information.

When reviewing a help system that uses information types, consider these questions:

- Are the information types appropriate for this application and its audience? This should be decided early in the planning phase, and can rarely be corrected at a late stage, but you can identify a problem for possible correction in the next release.

- Has each topic been assigned to the appropriate information type? Do some spot checking to see whether any major problems are evident. If possible, check every topic. Change any topics that are incorrectly assigned.

 "Information type" is an optional attribute you can assign to HTML Help topics, based on which users you want topics to reach; but you can use the same idea with other help systems. If a topic has no information type associated with it, it will always appear. See the help file for the HTML Help Workshop, or your help-authoring tool, for details on how to do this.

Choosing delivery methods

You can choose from a wide range of methods to deliver the help topics to users. Some methods require more coordination with programmers than other methods do. Choose methods that suit the product and its audience. Keep in mind that a method that some users like may be very irritating to others (Microsoft Office's Office Assistant—"Clippy"—is a well-known example).

 Don't spend so much time working on delivery methods that you forget, or don't have time, to write and organize good, useful information to deliver. Sometimes the simplest methods are the most effective—and the most appreciated by users.

Embedded help

Embedded help is designed to provide the information that users need without their having to ask for it. Some examples:

- Build help into the interface. For example, instead of displaying "Zip code" as a field label, display "Zip code (five digits, or five dash four)". Another technique is to include a few words or a brief set of instructions. "Click a book, and then click Open. Or click another tab, such as Index."

- Include screentips, tooltips, mouseovers, or small messages at the bottom of the application window (for example, in the status bar), that change depending on the location of the cursor. This sort of help is similar to *What's this?* help, but it's easier to use.

- Design the help window to always be open beside or below the application window and to display help related to whatever the user is doing at the time. This method can be useful for providing procedural help. This technique is *not* the one used in Microsoft Office 2000, where the application window resizes when the help is displayed.

Several of these types of help can be intrusive (and, in some applications, may take up valuable space on the screen); so, if possible, provide ways for users to hide the embedded help if they don't want it.

Most types of embedded help require work on the part of the programmers, so you must get agreement from the software developers early in the project.

Assistance for novice users

Assistance for novice users can take several forms, including wizards, coaches, show-me topics, and interactive tutorials. Some of these may also be suitable for helping experienced users perform a rarely-done task.

 When choosing any of the following types of assistance, keep in mind that what works quickly when installed on the user's machine—FlashHelp, for example—may be slow (or unavailable) if the user must download it from the Web.

The design and writing of wizards, coaches, and tutorials, and the integration of these features with the software, is outside the scope of this book. See Appendix C, "For More Information," for some relevant publications.

Show-me topics

Show-me topics demonstrate an action rather than merely describing it; for example, finding the location of an item on a submenu. Show-me help can be animated or static. Static help is typically a partial screen shot with an arrow or circle indicating the required item; the screen shot must show enough context so the user can find the item easily in the software interface.

Show-me help is often reached through a link in a procedural topic (see **Figure 3**), thus giving easy access to details that would irritate readers who don't need the information, and requiring no special programming; writers can do all that is necessary.

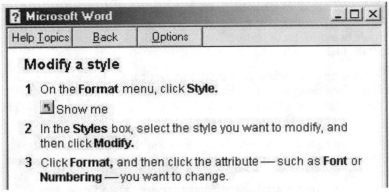

Figure 3. Example of a "Show me" link in a procedural topic.

Coaches

Coaches give users instruction on one step of a procedure, and the users perform this step in the software itself. If users need help with the next step, they can click a button on the coach window to go to the next page of instructions.

Coaches are useful for helping users work through complex, multi-dialog procedures and other situations that do not fit well into a single help topic.

Tutorials

Interactive tutorials provide environments in which users can practice procedures or experiment with data and results, without worrying about messing up their real data.

Writers can provide tutorials that users can select from within a procedure. An easier method is to provide an item on the Help menu, which users can select to go directly to a list of available tutorials. The ideal situation is to have a master list available from the Help menu and to have a link from the application dialog (or the procedural help for that dialog) when you're doing a task for which there's a tutorial.

Wizards

Wizards act as a combination of a help system and a software interface. Wizards step users through a series of actions and choices to help them accomplish a complex task. Users make choices and enter real data into a wizard, and they can cancel the process any time before finishing it. If you include wizards, provide some way for advanced users to turn them off or bypass them, and provide help for the pages of the wizards themselves.

Figure 4 shows an example of one page in a wizard. The page does not include enough information for novice users to understand the consequences of their choices, but it does have a Help button, which displays the topic shown in **Figure 5**.

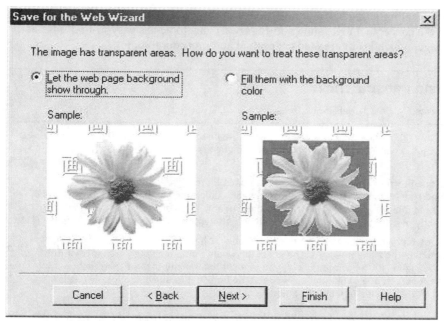

Figure 4. Example of one page of a wizard from Microsoft Image Composer.

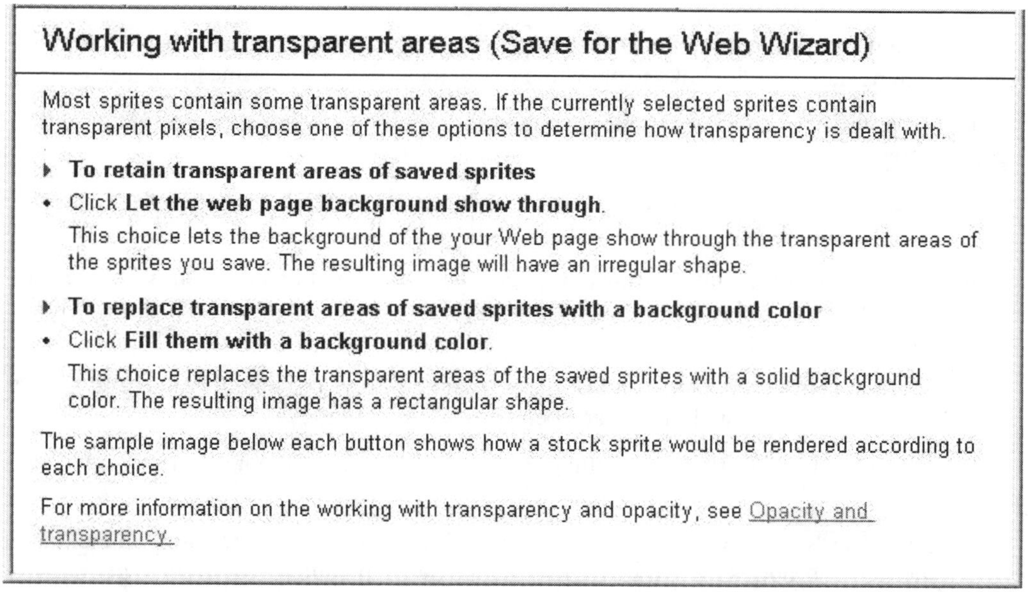

Working with transparent areas (Save for the Web Wizard)

Most sprites contain some transparent areas. If the currently selected sprites contain transparent pixels, choose one of these options to determine how transparency is dealt with.

▶ **To retain transparent areas of saved sprites**
• Click **Let the web page background show through**.
This choice lets the background of the your Web page show through the transparent areas of the sprites you save. The resulting image will have an irregular shape.

▶ **To replace transparent areas of saved sprites with a background color**
• Click **Fill them with a background color**.
This choice replaces the transparent areas of the saved sprites with a solid background color. The resulting image has a rectangular shape.

The sample image below each button shows how a stock sprite would be rendered according to each choice.

For more information on the working with transparency and opacity, see Opacity and transparency.

Figure 5. Help topic associated with wizard page shown in Figure 4.

Those users wanting to understand the concepts can click the link in the last paragraph, which displays the conceptual topic shown in **Figure 6**. This topic has easy-to-find links at the top of the page, which lead to related conceptual and procedural topics.

Opacity and transparency

▦ Related Topics   ▦ Overview   ▦ How?

The shape of a sprite is determined by the opacity of the image being represented and by the transparent space around it. However, the transparency of a sprite is not limited to the space surrounding it.

A sprite is defined by four channels that contain settings for red, green, blue, and alpha. The red, green, and blue channels define the amount of each color used in the sprite from 0 (none of the color used) to 255 (maximum amount of the color used). The alpha channel defines the degree of opacity of a sprite from zero (completely transparent) to 100 (completely opaque).

You can use the alpha channel as if it were another color. Many effects contain a setting for opacity, which sets the transparency of the effect anywhere from completely transparent (0%) to completely opaque (100%). For example, you can set the opacity of the **Erase** tool to partially erase a portion or a sprite and allow the sprite behind it to show through. The following is a composition that makes use of transparency.

Figure 6. Help topic displayed from the link in the last paragraph of Figure 5.

When reviewing show-me topics, coaches, tutorials, and wizards, consider these questions:

- Are the links to all the topics of a specific type presented in the same way? For example, are all the links to show-me topics identified by the same graphic?

- Does the help give unambiguous context for each item, so the user can find it on the interface?

- If a control described in one of these help topics is not available or not visible under some conditions, does the topic say what those conditions are?

- Do tutorials give a clear indication of how long they might take to run, what the user will learn, how to run them, how to quit, and whether users can return to the place where they stopped?

- Are the controls (Forward and Back, or Next and Previous) unambiguous and always located in the same place on each page?

- Are users told clearly that anything they do in a tutorial will not affect their real data?

- Do wizards have enough explanation on each page to assist novice users in making a decision? If not, is there a way—for example, a Help button—for users to get more information without closing the wizard?

Providing for users' preferences

A good help system should provide ways for users to skip simplified explanations and other features if they don't want them. Some suggestions:

- Be sure to include more than just procedural help topics in your help system. Other topic types include overviews, concepts, reference, problem-solving, and error message help. See "Content of topic types" in Chapter 3, "Developing Specifications," for more information on topic types.

- Group topics in the table of contents by user or topic type. An example is shown in Figure 1.

- Use information types and let users choose what level they want.

- Provide ways for users to keep help on top of or beside the application, or to hide the help. In WinHelp, for example, items can be provided on the Options menu of the Help file, as shown in **Figure 7**. Check the documentation for your help system or authoring tool, to see what your choices are.

- Provide ways to turn off some features of the help. For example, although wizards and related features can be very helpful to novice users, more experienced users often find them intrusive and irritating. **Figure 8** shows an example from Microsoft Publisher, which provides options for users to turn off specific features.

- Use conditional help, where individual users can specify their preferences (and change them whenever they wish). Methods for providing conditional help will vary with the type of help and the tools available. For an HTML-based help system, writers could use cookies and a bit of JavaScript to program the conditions, without needing to involve the software programmers.

  Dave Gash of HyperTrain dot Com provides a simple demonstration of the technique. **Figure 9** shows the Welcome page presented to users when they first open a help system. The choices made here are stored in a cookie on the user's computer; from now on, the help system will display the type of help requested, in the font size requested, with the user's preferred background color. Other preferences could be similarly coded. (At any time, users can return to this page and change preferences.)

  For details on this technique, and the coding involved, visit Resources | Smart Help on Dave Gash's Web site, **http://www.hypertrain.com/**.

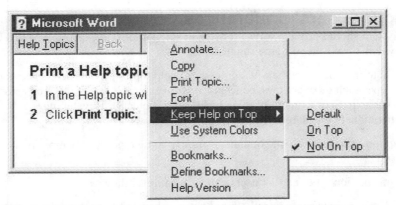

Figure 7. Choices for displaying help can be on the Options menu.

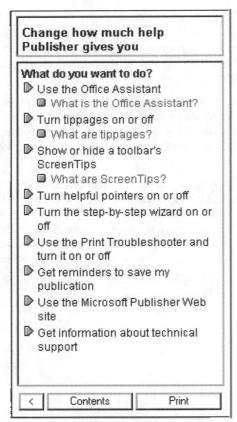

Figure 8. Example of a help topic with options to turn off specific features.

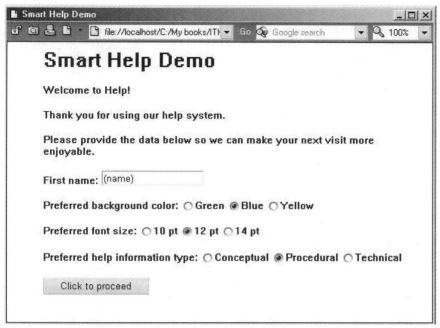

Figure 9. Example of the input page for a smart help system.

Integrating the help system with other documents and systems

Help systems can be used in conjunction with other forms of user assistance, such as electronic performance support systems (EPSS) and other types of online documents, including PDF files, Web-based systems, and company intranets. Refer to Appendix C for more information.

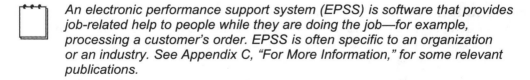

An electronic performance support system (EPSS) is software that provides job-related help to people while they are doing the job—for example, processing a customer's order. EPSS is often specific to an organization or an industry. See Appendix C, "For More Information," for some relevant publications.

If other documents and systems are available to users, a help system ideally will be integrated with those other systems. Integrated systems need to be planned in advance, to ensure that provision is made for any programming work required; that necessary files are shipped with the product; that writing style, terminology, and other details are consistent across the help and other documents or EPSS; and that appropriate linking can be made from the help system.

At a minimum, the help system should tell users where to find more information. Quick programming fixes include putting an item on a Help menu that links to Web-based information. Writers can also make quick fixes by inserting links from help topics to Web pages or other files. Tools are available for linking to specific pages in PDF files.

 Keep in mind that some users—for example, staff using a laptop when traveling, or people on dial-up Internet connections—may not have instant access to other documents and systems that are not on the hard disk of their own computers. You need to warn users that a link goes to the Web.

Some questions to ask when reviewing integrated help systems:

- Do the links lead users to relevant information?

- Do links to the Web make it clear that's where they go?

- Is vital information installed on the user's system, or are users forced to go to other sources (a potential problem)?

- Should some information be moved from other files to the help system?

- Should some information be moved from the help system to other files? For example, conceptual information might go better in an online reference manual.

- Can PDF files or other relevant documents be opened outside the application? For example, troubleshooting information could be placed in a file that is accessible when the application isn't working.

Avoiding common problems

A good time to diagnose and avoid many potential problems is at the detailed prototype stage (see "Building a detailed contents prototype" in Chapter 4, "Prototyping the Help System"). When evaluating the prototype help, test your questions against the help topics.

Later, as you begin writing the help topics, check a sample for symptoms of not enough detail, too much detail, or the wrong level of detail. Refine your writing based on the results of the sample.

Not enough detail

Too little detail often occurs because the writer didn't have the information, didn't think to include it, or didn't think any explanation was necessary.

Here are some symptoms of too little detail:

- The help contains obvious information or instructions, or topics that repeat what's on the dialog itself, with no further information.

  Example. "Type the customer's name in the *Customer name* field" gives no indication of the maximum number of characters, case sensitivity, or whether accented or other non-English characters can be included.

  Example. For a date field, if the user interface doesn't indicate what format is required, the help should say more than "Type the invoice date here."

- Ambiguous words are not explained. Not everyone uses common English words exactly the way you do; regional and international conventions can vary quite a bit. For example, "title" can mean "Mr., Ms., Mrs., Dr." or it can mean a job title such as Manager or Technical Writer, which others might call "position" or "role."

- Lots of jargon is unexplained, suggesting that the material might require more prior knowledge than at least some of the audience is likely to have.

- No indication is given of where users can get information they need to type in, when this could be provided—for example, for in-house systems that automate company procedures.

- No indication is given of how to recover from errors, or what to do if something doesn't work as described. In many cases, this is a symptom of problems in the user interface, particularly with cryptic error messages.

  Example. An error message like "You cannot delete this customer" leaves the user wondering "Why not? Not now or not ever? Can someone else, with a different authority level, do it for me?" If the help doesn't answer these questions, it lacks appropriate detail.

- No indication is provided of a control's purpose or when it should be used, although "how to operate it" is explained.

Too much detail

Too much detail often occurs because writers assume all users need this level of detail, or they don't know how to subdivide it. Here are some symptoms of too much detail:

- Long, complex procedures often contain subprocedures, or branching procedures with every "what if" included. "If xxx, go to step 11. If xxx, go to step 22." See **Figure 10** for an example.

- Long, scrolling topics contain several types of information (conceptual, procedural, reference).

- Paragraphs of explanation are intermixed with procedural steps. A relevant explanation introducing a series of steps is valuable; digressions usually are not.

- Several overlapping ideas are included in one topic, instead of in related topics.

- Step-by-step instructions are provided for obvious "fill in the blanks" situations, with no relevant explanations.

  Example. "Type the customer's last name in the Last Name field. Type the customer's first name in the First Name field. Type the customer's street address in the Address field." This example combines too much irrelevant detail with a lack of relevant information, such as whether the fields are case-sensitive or have a limit on the number of characters.

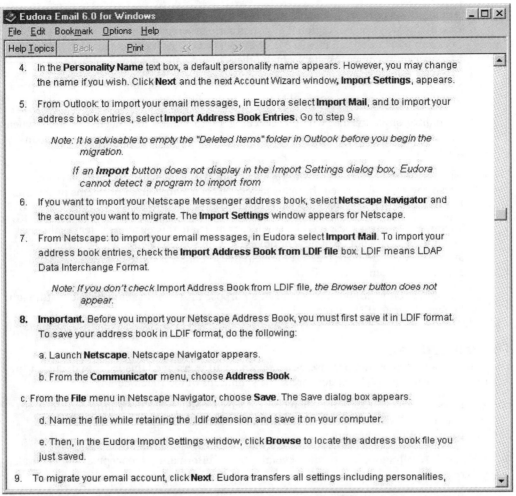

Figure 10. Example of a branching procedure containing a subprocedure (and other problems). Note that step 8 should be done before step 7; steps 5 and 7 are alternatives, not sequential, with step 9 following from either of them; and steps 6 and 7 seem to contradict, or possibly duplicate, each other.

- Topics include digressions into the workings of the system, the derivation of field contents, or any other subject not of immediate relevance. Sometimes, what appears to be a digression may be an important and relevant technical detail that the user must understand before making a decision. In most cases, however, the digression—although it may contain valuable information—is not relevant at that place or in that topic. Misplaced valuable information should be moved to another place, either in the same topic or in a separate topic. **Figure 11** and **Figure 12** (from Dave Gash, HyperTrain dot Com) show a before-and-after example.

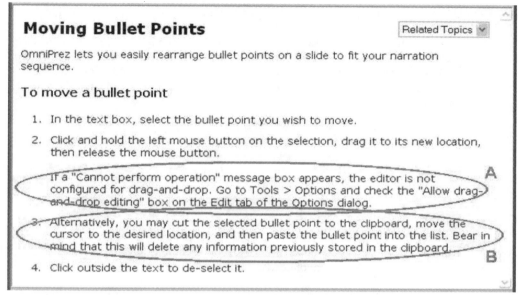

Figure 11. Example of a procedure containing digressions. (A) is a separate troubleshooting procedure; (B) is an alternative procedure.

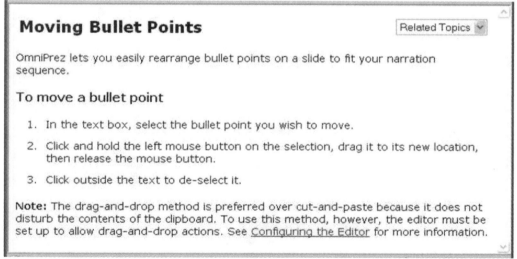

Figure 12. Procedure from Figure 11, with digressions removed to a separate topic.

- Everything, including how to use the operating system, is described in detail, even when the audience can be expected to have prior knowledge, or when something is completely irrelevant to the topic. For example, "click the left mouse button" instead of "click," or—even worse—"position your mouse cursor on the button and click the left mouse button." For most audiences, such detail is not required; if you believe part of the audience needs that information, put it in a separate topic, not in every procedure.

- Many pop-up topics are included within procedural topics, when "see also" or "related topics" links are more appropriate. Pop-up topics can be very distracting or annoying if overused.

- There is no easy way to find out more about a topic at an overview level.

Conclusion

User assistance for software needs to provide suitable levels of detail for a range of users, from novices to experts. This chapter has looked at many of the techniques available for designing and delivering help that meets a range of needs.

Updates and corrections to this chapter can be found on Hentzenwerke's Web site, **www.hentzenwerke.com**. Click "Catalog" and navigate to the page for this book.

Chapter 9
Linking from Application to Help

Linking from the application to the help requires cooperation with programmers, as well as consideration of users' needs. This chapter describes different ways of linking, the pros and cons of each, and the type of information that writers and programmers need to share to make the system work.

During the planning phase of your help project, writers and programmers need to agree on the type and extent of linking and who specifies the identifiers that are used to link the application to the help file. Ensure that the details of this agreement are in the help plan or specifications. Problems often arise when these details are not agreed to in advance, or when the programmers belatedly change the way they are doing the linking. Here are some questions to ask during the planning process:

- At what level of detail will the help be linked to the application? Will the help always open at the table of contents—not recommended—or will specific topics be assigned to individual dialogs or fields (context-sensitive help)? This chapter assumes you will be providing some type of context-sensitive help.

- What controls on the application's user interface will be used to display different types of help topics?

- How will help topics be displayed? HTML-based help displayed in a browser is often quite different from standard WinHelp or HTML Help.

- If the application contains dialogs with several tabs, or dialogs that display different fields depending on circumstances, how will the help be linked to those dialogs? Will each tab, or each variation of a dynamic dialog, be linked to its own help topic, or will only one topic be linked? See "Providing help for dynamic (variable) dialogs" and "Providing help for dialogs with multiple tabs" later in this chapter.

- Who will specify which help topic to link to which item in the application? (Writers should do this.) See "Using topic IDs and context numbers" later in this chapter.

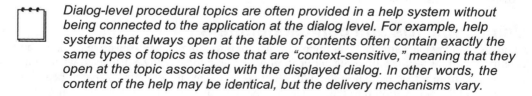

Dialog-level procedural topics are often provided in a help system without being connected to the application at the dialog level. For example, help systems that always open at the table of contents often contain exactly the same types of topics as those that are "context-sensitive," meaning that they open at the topic associated with the displayed dialog. In other words, the content of the help may be identical, but the delivery mechanisms vary.

Although the decisions about what items to link to help topics can sometimes be complicated, the actual coding of the links between the software and the help system is usually straightforward. Programmers provide numeric identifiers for each dialog and field, writers provide alphanumeric identifiers for each help topic, and together they produce a file that "maps" the help topics to the corresponding dialogs or fields. (Your help-authoring tool may be able to do most of the work for you, although you'll need to make the decisions.) For more about this process, see "Using topic IDs and context numbers" later in this chapter.

Other sections of this chapter look at some of the issues related to the decisions required.

Providing context-sensitive help

The term *context-sensitive help* has two main meanings: help provided at dialog (or window) level, and help provided at field level. Be sure that writers and programmers agree on what they mean by the term. Write the definition into the help plan and the help specifications.

Ideally, you'll provide both dialog-level help and field-level help in the same help system, by using:

- The Help button, the F1 key, or a similar mechanism to display dialog-level help.

- Some other mechanism to display field-level help. For example, on Windows systems, users might click a question mark button, then click inside the field. In Web-based applications, users might click on the field name or rest the mouse cursor on the field.

Dialog-level (window-level) help

Dialog-level or window-level help displays a topic specific to the active dialog or window. This topic is often procedural—describing the tasks users can perform using the dialog or window. From the help window, users should be able to access the contents page, index, and other navigational features of the help. The topic may contain links to related conceptual or reference topics; it may also provide information about all the fields, or links to field-level topics. This level of help is most suitable for situations where some explanation of the dialog is needed, particularly for novice users.

Field-level help

Field-level help displays a topic for each object (field, button, other controls) in a dialog or window. The topic may be presented in a pop-up window, a secondary window, or the main help window. This level of help is most suitable for situations where it's obvious what's going on in the dialog, but the user may be unsure about field details such as date formats, case-sensitivity, or the consequences of choices. (Often, much of this field-level information can be provided on the user interface.)

Using topic IDs and context numbers

Choosing display mechanisms is an important part of providing context-sensitive help, but an equally important task is telling the application which help topic is to be displayed when help is requested from a specific dialog, field, or other control. This information is shared between the help and the application through the use of topic IDs, dialog and field IDs, and a list or file that "maps" the help topic IDs to the corresponding dialog and field IDs.

- Each help topic has a unique alphanumeric identifier, which may be called a *topic ID* or some similar name. For HTML (Web) pages, the file name—or a named anchor within the page—is used as the topic ID. Examples of topic IDs are "IDH_PRINTGRAPH" or "Printing_a_graph" for WinHelp and Microsoft HTML Help, or "myfile.htm#anchor-name" for Web pages. Topic IDs may be assigned automatically by help-authoring tools, or writers can assign them manually.

- Each dialog in a software application has a unique numeric identifier, which may be called a *context number*, *help ID*, or some similar name. This identifier is defined in the program's source files. Examples of dialog IDs are 205 and 40319. Fields and controls may also have numeric IDs, if programmers have included them.

Mapping of the two sets of identifiers can be done in several ways, only one of which is described here. This method is recommended because it ensures that writers, not programmers, decide which topic is called from which dialog or field in the application.

1. The programmer should provide the writer with a list of the context numbers (dialog and field IDs) used in the application, along with sufficient information to tell the writer which dialog or control is associated with each ID.

2. The writer can use a help-authoring tool to generate a header file containing all the alphanumeric topic IDs, and then add the numeric IDs (provided by the programmer) to the appropriate topics in the map file.

3. For any topics that are not intended to be directly connected to the application (for example, conceptual topics), the writer assigns a numeric identifier that is not already in use.

Listing 1 shows an example of a map file for a WinHelp or HTML Help project. The map file used in your project may differ in appearance.

Listing 1. Part of a map file (filename.h) for a WinHelp or HTML Help project.

```
[MAP]
#define Adding_a_new_report_view_to_a_report_book    109
#define Adding_pictures_to_a_report    185
#define Adv_button      42
#define Alignment       269
#define Alignment_dialog        247
#define APN_checkbox    32
#define Applied_filters_list    24
#define Apply_button    114
#define Area_Lines_checkbox     123
#define Auto_shell      186
#define Autolink        154
#define Available_items_list    28
#define Back_Color_button       274
#define Border 272
#define Borders_button          69
#define Borders_checkbox        121
#define Bottom_rows_of_tabs_graph       279
#define Bottom_Tab      144
#define Cancel_button 115
```

Solving context-sensitive help complications

Occasionally, you'll run into complications writing context-sensitive help, and you'll need to find creative solutions to problems like these:

- Some dialogs are dynamic; that is, the fields and controls on them change depending on the circumstances.

- Some dialogs have numerous tabs, requiring long topics to cover everything.

- The help will be linked only at the dialog level, not the field level.

Providing help for dynamic (variable) dialogs

Many programs use dynamic dialogs, in which the available fields and controls vary depending on what the user is doing. Dynamic dialogs come in two main types:

- Dialogs in which one selection affects the other fields, controls, and selections now available to the user. In this case, some items may become unavailable (but still be visible); other items may not be visible.

- Dialogs that vary depending on what the user was previously doing; that is, from which other dialog the user reached the one in question. In this case, one dialog may show different fields in different situations, the title may change, and the defaults may vary.

Users typically won't know that the dialog has changed; instead, they will think it's a different dialog, because they were doing something different when they reached it. Ideally, dialog-level help for each version of a dynamic dialog would be a separate topic, so users see only information about the fields and controls that are visible (whether or not they are available for use), and not the ones that are hidden. In most cases, however, writers will need to provide one help topic that addresses all possible variations.

For the first type of dynamic dialog (with variable fields), one way to write the help is shown in **Figure 1**. The topic explains what happens to the fields when certain selections are made in the dialog. This help system is linked at the dialog level only, so the topic includes field help in the form of clickable hotspots on a graphic. **Figure 2** shows a pop-up description for a field that is not always displayed on the dialog. The field information could also be provided in a separate (perhaps secondary) help window.

To deal with the second type of dynamic dialog (that varies depending on the dialog from which the user reached this one), help writers and editors need to understand exactly how many times it can appear in different guises, and exactly how different these instances are.

If the differences are minor, one help topic may be able to cover all instances in general terms, similar to the solution for the first type of dynamic dialog.

If the differences are great (from the users' point of view), one possible solution is to explain that this dialog is reused in different situations and to list the variations of the dialog —perhaps as a list of user tasks. Each item in the list of variations or tasks can then be linked to another topic that provides full dialog-level help for that instance of the dialog.

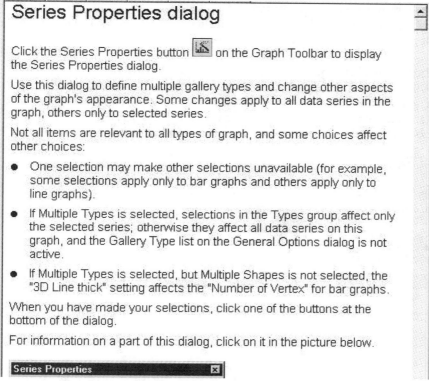

Figure 1. *Top part of a sample help topic for a dialog with variable fields.*

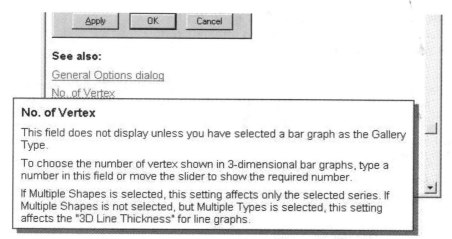

Figure 2. *A continuation of the sample help topic in Figure 1.*

The biggest problem for writers, particularly with poorly specified programs (or those that undergo rapid, undocumented changes during development), is to recognize the existence of dynamic dialogs so that you can write appropriate help.

Providing help for dialogs with multiple tabs

Many programs use dialogs with multiple tabs. If one help topic is associated with the entire dialog, it needs to provide help for each tab. To avoid a long, scrolling topic, writers can provide a general topic with links to topics about the individual tabs, as shown in **Figure 3**. The help topic for each tab should contain links to help for the other tabs.

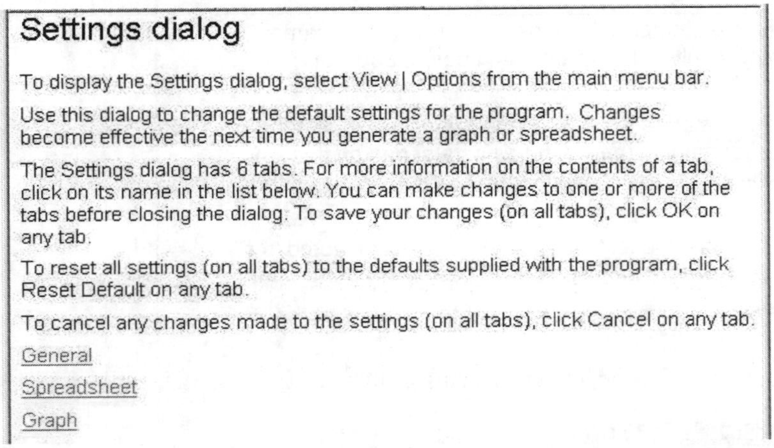

Settings dialog

To display the Settings dialog, select View | Options from the main menu bar.

Use this dialog to change the default settings for the program. Changes become effective the next time you generate a graph or spreadsheet.

The Settings dialog has 6 tabs. For more information on the contents of a tab, click on its name in the list below. You can make changes to one or more of the tabs before closing the dialog. To save your changes (on all tabs), click OK on any tab.

To reset all settings (on all tabs) to the defaults supplied with the program, click Reset Default on any tab.

To cancel any changes made to the settings (on all tabs), click Cancel on any tab.

General

Spreadsheet

Graph

Figure 3. Sample help topic written for a multi-tab dialog. Links jump to individual help topics for each tab on the dialog. Figure 4 shows the help topic for one tab.

Providing field-level help within dialog-level help

Sometimes you can't provide field-level help that is directly accessible from the fields themselves, but you can provide dialog-level help. In such a case, you can link to field-level help from the dialog-level help topics by using one of several techniques:

- Use a definition list or table to provide the field information in the dialog-level topic itself. This method has the advantage that the user can print out the entire topic with all the field information included. For example:

  Field 1 name
  Description of field 1

  Field 2 name
  Description of field 2

  or

  Field 1 name   Description of field 1

  Field 2 name   Description of field 2

- Put the field names in a simple list, and link each name to a pop-up topic. This method saves space but does not allow the field information to be printed with the rest of the topic.

- Put the field names in a simple list and use expanding sections to display explanations (see "Using expanding sections" in Chapter 7, "Providing Navigation and Context"). This method saves space, but also allows the user to print out the entire topic with all the field information included.

- Include a screen capture of the dialog. Place hotspots (clickable areas) on the fields in the graphic, and have each hotspot link to a topic about that field. The field-level topics can be in pop-up, secondary, or full windows, depending on the length and complexity of the topic. **Figure 4** shows an example.

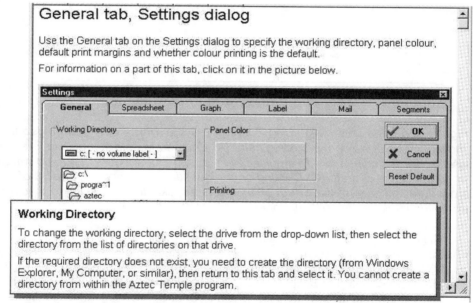

Figure 4. Help topic for one page of a multi-tab dialog, showing a pop-up topic that is displayed when the user clicks a specific area of the screen shot.

Providing context-sensitive help for Web pages

The principles of providing context-sensitive help for Web pages are the same as for other applications, but the technical details of the display mechanisms are different. A full discussion of the possibilities is outside the scope of this book. See Appendix C, "For More Information," for some references on HTML, XML, JavaScript, and others.

Before you enthusiastically embrace all the features available to you, stop and consider accessibility issues. Make sure that your help doesn't depend upon features that some users won't see. In addition to considering the needs of users with disabilities or those on slow connections, remember that many companies block pop-ups or scripting in Web pages. See Appendix C, "For More Information," for some references about accessibility.

Figure 5 demonstrates some of the ways that you could provide dialog and field help for a Web page.

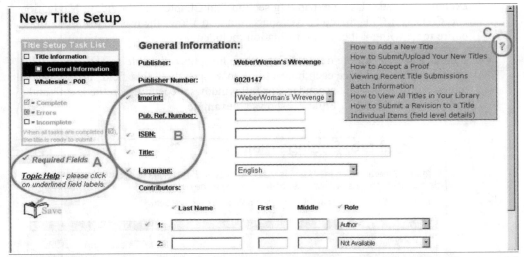

Figure 5. A page on the Lightning Source Web site, http://www.lightningsource.com/, showing several ways of providing help. (A) Embedded help instructions are always visible. (B) Underlined words are links to field help that appears in pop-up windows when the link is clicked. (C) Clicking on the question mark pops up the list of procedures as shown; each item on the list is a clickable link leading to a pop-up window containing the full help topic.

The links in the (B) circle in Figure 5 could be provided in a variety of ways, several of which involve JavaScript coding, which may not be available to all users. You could also provide a simple link (`<a href="pagename.htm">Field name</a>`) to another Web page, for those without JavaScript—not an elegant solution, but certainly a workable one.

The pop-up from the question mark graphic (C) uses JavaScript, although the items in the list can be simple links. Again, the JavaScript link could have an alternative simple link that would display the list on a separate Web page.

Figure 6 shows three types of field help and one link to dialog help on another Web page on the Lightning Source site, **http://www.lightningsource.com/**.

Details of coding the links from a Web page to the help are the responsibility of the programmer. They are mentioned here so you will have an idea of the possibilities.

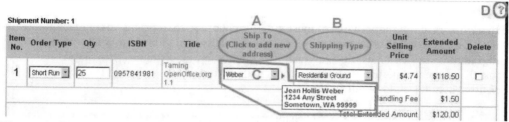

Figure 6. Examples of field-level help for a Web page. (A) Link to a separate page for adding addresses. (B) Link to a page of information about shipping types. (C) Pop-up details for selection in associated field. (D) Pops up a list of procedures (not shown here); each list item is a clickable link.

Identifying common linking problems

Most linking problems are user interface issues, and therefore they are the programmers' responsibility. However, if linking problems are not fixed, writers may need to find creative ways to overcome them.

When reviewing or testing the help with a working application, here are some problems to look for:

- There is no Help button or other way to get help from a dialog or wizard. Writers may be unable to do anything about this problem other than to point out the usability issues, but testing or QA may have more authority to get the problem fixed.

- Help always opens at field level. In some applications, this arrangement may be appropriate for the audience; in others, it may confuse novice users who want to know what's going on at the dialog level. Again, writers may be unable to do anything about this problem except point it out and hope QA supports their opinion.

- Help opens a topic that seems irrelevant. This problem is most likely a mapping issue, which can be fixed by the writer.

- Similar dialogs that arise in different situations but share one help topic, which either does not make sense in each situation, is too brief and general, without links to specific topics for each situation, or is long and complex. The writer is responsible for rewording or dividing the help topic.

If time and resources do not permit programming solutions, here are some things that writers can do on their own:

- If help always opens at the contents page or index, improve them, as discussed in Chapter 6, "Producing the Table of Contents and Index."

- If help always opens at field-level topics, link back from them to dialog-level topics.

Conclusion

Programmers and writers share responsibility for choosing appropriate linking techniques and making them work. Writers may have to produce creative solutions to problems that programmers can't—or won't—solve through programming changes. This chapter has looked at some techniques for linking from an application to the help, to provide context-sensitive help for dialogs and fields.

Updates and corrections to this chapter can be found on Hentzenwerke's Web site, **www.hentzenwerke.com**. Click "Catalog" and navigate to the page for this book.

Chapter 10
Copyediting and Production Editing

Copyediting should go beyond correcting grammar and punctuation to revising the language used and the presentation of the material, to ensure it meets the requirements in the specifications and style guide. Production editing is done at the end of the development phase, checking that the topics in the help system display as they should, and that the navigation works properly.

Editing is an essential part of the writing process. Writers usually edit their own drafts, but someone else should always edit their work as well. No matter how skilled writers are, they are too familiar with the material to see all the problems it may have. It's especially difficult to spot what's missing in your own work—that essential bit of information that you know so well, you forget to mention it.

Editing is frequently divided into three broad categories:

- Substantive editing—deals with the overall structure of the help; should be done early in the development of the help system and at various stages during development

- Copyediting—deals with writing style, consistency, grammar, and other issues; should be done at various stages during help development

- Production editing (sometimes called quality editing)—generally done as the last step before final production

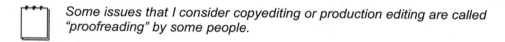 *Some issues that I consider copyediting or production editing are called "proofreading" by some people.*

Ideally, each type of editing is done by a skilled and experienced editor, who is familiar with the use of style guides and specifications and the particular requirements of online help. If you don't have a suitably experienced editor available, peer editing (by another writer) is your next best choice. In some cases, another coworker or your manager can be quite helpful in spotting inconsistencies and unclear writing. Unfortunately, some inexperienced editors can also waste a lot of the writer's time; if they aren't familiar with—and willing to follow—the help specifications and style guide, they may attempt to make inappropriate changes.

It's also very important to distinguish between the roles of technical reviewers—who are looking for inaccurate information—and copyeditors, who should be looking primarily at the writing itself. Although one person can fill the roles of both reviewer and editor, avoid having someone do both at the same time. Many people trying to fill both roles tend to focus too closely on writing issues and forget to look at the technical accuracy of the material.

This chapter summarizes general copyediting and production editing issues and focuses on special problems with online help. See "How many reviews are needed, and when?" and "Methods for reviewing and testing" in Chapter 1, "Planning an Online Help Project," for related information on some practical aspects of editing.

Defining editorial roles

Because of the diversity of ideas and definitions about editors' roles, you need to clarify exactly what the editor is expected to do, regardless of who does the editing. For example, what does the editor mean by the term *copyediting*? It may be rather different from what you mean. The editor may think it includes a lot more revising of language use than you expect, or that it includes testing the help against the product and evaluating its helpfulness.

 You need to clarify what editing will be done, when, by whom, and how. Include a detailed description of the editor's role, responsibility, and authority in the help plan. For example, do the writers treat a copyeditor's comments as suggestions or requirements?

Several schemes have been devised to help define editors' roles. One is the "types and levels of edit" concept summarized in a paper by Robert van Buren and Mary Ann Buehler (1980), which divides editing into nine types, grouped into five levels. It emphasizes what I call "rule-based editing."

In 1999 the Council of Biology Editors published David E. Nadziejka's "Levels of Technical Editing," which argues that "...the primary editorial focus must be to help ensure that the technical content is complete, accurate, and understandable to the intended audience." The emphasis, he argues, should be on what I call "analysis-based editing," with formal grammatical correctness of secondary importance, when time is limited.

Rule-based and analysis-based edits

Classifying editing tasks into "rule-based" and "analysis-based" edits provides a basis for determining which editorial decisions are negotiable between the editor and the writer and which are non-negotiable.

Rule-based editing covers ways to make the help correct, consistent, accurate and complete, using a style guide. Rule-based editing is usually non-negotiable with the writer; the editor enforces the rules, as specified by the company. Some examples:

- Spelling, grammar, punctuation, capitalization, hyphenation

- Adherence to legal requirements (copyright, trademarks, and so on)

- Internal consistency, typically to do with design: typography, layout, and illustrations

- Bibliographic references and citations

But rule-based editing is not enough; the document can still be inappropriate for the intended audience.

Analysis-based editing covers the process of evaluating a document for concept, content, organization, form, and style, to make it more functional and appropriate for its readers.

Much of this type of editing should be negotiable: The editor can suggest improvements rather than make corrections.

Problems arise when the difference between "enforcing the rules" and "making suggestions" is not clear.

Substantive editing of online help

Substantive editing deals with the overall structure of the help. In the prototyping and early draft stages, and throughout the development of the help system, the editor should have been looking at the issues covered in Chapters 5 through 9 of this book. Substantive editing often overlaps with usability testing, which is described in more detail in Chapter 11, "Usability Testing on a Budget."

Substantive editing (also called *development editing* and *comprehensive editing*) is often done by a different person from the copyeditor. Substantive editors do not need to have as good a command of the language as copyeditors, but they do need to have excellent analytical and problem-solving skills.

In the absence of a substantive editor, a good copyeditor—if given enough time—should look at these issues in addition to those listed later:

- Does the help all fit together into a coherent whole?

- Is all the necessary information included, and unnecessary information deleted?

- Is the help helpful? Does the content answer the target audience's questions?

- Are the retrieval aids (particularly the index) useful?

- Are the navigation aids logical and useful in context? Can users easily find the links they want?

Copyediting online help

Much copyediting can be done on paper, particularly in early stages of the project when the editor is looking at draft topics. However, some issues must be checked online. I discuss the online issues in the "Production editing online help" section of this chapter, but many people consider them to be part of the copyediting step. You might use two people to copyedit: one to check the text on paper and another to check for online display problems.

When copyediting online help (on paper or online), you should look for most of the same problems that you would check in printed documents:

- Spelling

- Word use, including whether jargon or technical terms are appropriate for the audience

- Sentence complexity and use of active or passive verbs

- Conciseness

- Clear, logical development of ideas

- Consistent use of terms
- Consistent style and presentation of procedures and other topics
- Conformance to legal requirements
- Correct grammar and punctuation
- Correct, consistent use of bulleted or numbered lists
- List items in parallel style
- Illustrations correctly inserted
- Mathematical equations and special symbols presented correctly
- Consistent capitalization and punctuation
- Consistent use of bold, italics, color, or other highlighting

Look particularly for these problems:

- Topic titles unclear, misleading, too long, or not in required style
- Long, wordy sentences or paragraphs that should be turned into lists
- Long, complex, or branching procedures, or too many subprocedures
- Steps out of order in procedures
- Wording of explanations too technical or cryptic for the audience
- Link text unclear, misleading, too long, too short, or not in approved style
- Too many links, or links too close together
- Internal inconsistency—for example, references to items that don't exist in the help
- Incomprehensible statements (for example, resulting from missing material)
- Any other deviations from specifications

Some questions to ask when reviewing context-sensitive help:

- Is it appropriate for the audience and the product?
- Does it behave consistently? Does dialog-level help always open the same type of help, for example procedural? Sometimes consistency isn't necessary, but in most cases users will develop an expectation for what they'll find when they ask for help.
- Is it written consistently? For example, *What's this?* help might always begin with a verb, or dialog-level help might always begin with an infinitive sentence leading into a procedure.

If the help system is going to be localized for international markets, the copyeditor also needs to consider the issues covered in "How will the help meet localization criteria?" in Chapter 3, "Developing Specifications." This work may involve looking at more than one version of the compiled help.

When copyediting on screen, add the problems listed in "Production editing online help" later in this chapter. See also the checklists in Appendix E.

Example of accurate content requiring rewording

This example is taken from OpenOffice.org Writer, a word-processing program. In version 1.0.3, the online help for cross-referencing included the following instructions. (A broader explanation of cross-referencing appeared at the beginning of the description of the Fields – References dialog. This section describes one item on the dialog.)

Name

Enter the name of user-defined fields here. Set a target to give the field a name. If you then insert a reference to it, use the name that appears at the field type "Set reference" in the selection field to identify the target.

For references within the sub-documents of a master document, the name of a reference that is not in the same sub-document has to be entered manually.

Although the explanation is accurate, it's difficult for a novice user to understand.

Here is the revised wording from the help file for version 1.1.1 of the program. The functionality has not changed, but the explanation is better.

Name

Type the name of the user-defined field that you want to create. To set a target, click "Set Reference" in the Type list, type a name in this box, and then click Insert. To reference the new target, click the target name in the Selection list.

In a master document, targets that are in different sub-documents are not displayed in the Selection list. If you want to insert a reference to the target, you must type the path and the name in the Name box.

Although the second version of the help explanation is much better, it's still too short and cryptic for many users, because it tries to cover several different (though related) uses of the dialog. Here's my version of this passage.

Name

To specify some text (such as a heading) as a target for cross-referencing, first select the text. Then click "Set Reference" in the Type list and type an identifying word or phrase in the Name box.

To create a cross-reference to a previously defined target, click Insert Reference in the Type list, and then click the target's name in the Selection list. The name appears in the Name box.

In a master document, the names of targets that are in different sub-documents are not displayed in the Selection list. If you want to insert a reference to a target in a different sub-document, you must type the name of the target in the Name box. Note: Target names are case-sensitive.

Using a style guide

A style guide is a reference document that includes rules and suggestions for writing style and document presentation. Style guides often specify which choice to use when several choices exist, and they include items that are specific to the company or industry and items for which a "standard" example does not exist through commercial style guides. The specific content in the style guide often is not a matter of "correct" or "incorrect" grammar or style, but rather the decisions you or your employer or client have made from among the many possibilities.

More specifically, style guides can serve several purposes:

- To ensure that documents conform to corporate image and policy, including legal requirements

- To inform new writers and editors of existing style and presentation decisions and solutions

- To define which style issues are negotiable and which are not

- To improve consistency within and among documents, especially when more than one writer is involved or when a document will be translated

- To remove the necessity to reinvent the wheel for every new project

- To remind the writer of style decisions for each project, when one writer works on several projects that have different style requirements

- To serve as part of the specifications for the deliverables

A style guide contains both rules (non-negotiable) and suggestions or recommendations (negotiable). Which items should be rules and which should be suggestions is a matter of opinion and corporate policy, though items that result from audience analysis and usability testing are more objective and thus more likely to be rules.

Style guides often contain three types of information, two of which should be in other documents:

- Process (how we do things in this company or this department).
  Process information should be in the help plan, or in a process guide referenced by the help plan, not in a style guide.

- Design (appearance of the online help).
  Design information should be in the help specifications, not in a style guide.

- Style (contents of the help; writing style).

What belongs in a style guide?

A style guide should be an evolving document. Don't change the rules halfway through a project, but do add items to the style guide when you make a decision to resolve an inconsistency or solve some other writing problem.

Try to make your style guide cover as many relevant issues as you can, without turning it into a writing tutorial. Some of the items I've listed for a style guide might be put somewhere else in your help specifications.

A style guide (or other subset of the specifications) should include the answers to questions like these:

- What version of English to use (American? British? Australian? Indian?), specifying any variations. For example, in Australia, when writing online help for the local market, it's common to use Australian English but spell computer-specific terms (such as *program* or *disk*) in the industry-standard way rather than the generic way (*programme, disc*).

- What system of measurement to use (metric? American?), specifying any variations (for example, dots per inch) and whether conversions should be included in parentheses. If conversions are included, make sure to confirm them with an appropriate expert and to indicate how many decimal places the conversion requires for acceptable accuracy.

- Any primary source materials (such as an industry style guide, a particular dictionary, the company's design and process guides) to use, specifying any variations. Don't reinvent the wheel when suitable wheels already exist; focus on the things that are unique to your company or product.

- What document elements (for example, table of contents, index, summary of changes, copyright and trademark information, glossary) are required, and what goes in them.

- Which template to use for each type of help topic. (Content templates might be part of the detailed specifications.)

- What style of capitalization to use for headings, vertical lists, figure and table captions, and other situations.

- What style of punctuation to use for running lists, vertical lists, and other situations.

- What style to use for cross-references or clickable links within the help and to other documents.

- When to use various types of highlighting (for example, bold or italic type).

- Whether illustrations and tables always need captions. If not, when do they need captions and when don't they? Should they always be referenced in the text? If not, under what circumstances can a reference be omitted? How should captions be punctuated?

- When to spell out numbers and when to use numerals; the use of commas, spaces, or other punctuation in numbers over 999.

- Word use (for example, company-specific, platform-specific, or product-specific terms; acronyms and abbreviations; and words to be avoided).

- Acceptable jargon, and the spelling, capitalization, and hyphenation of names and terms. Abbreviations used, including in measurements.

- Use of limited English, if relevant—for example, for translation efficiency or when the target audience is known to have limited knowledge of English.

- Wording, usage, and highlighting of caution, danger, and warning notices.

- Index style: how many levels? General guidelines on deciding what goes into an index, or reference another document containing this information. Guidelines on wording of index entries.

- Glossaries, bibliographies, and footnotes: what style, and when to use.

- How to indicate and acknowledge trademarks.

- Writing style, including reader-centered and task-oriented, using active voice and imperative mood ("Do this, then do that.")

Company and project style guides

If your company has a company style guide, it may cover issues that apply to all the company's technical publications, but it may not have sufficient detail for a help project. (A small company with only a few main product lines may have a company style guide that covers all products.) You may need to supplement a company style guide with a project style guide (often called a *style sheet*, not to be confused with a *cascading style sheet* or *CSS* in Web development) that records any decisions made for a particular project, especially on issues that are not covered by the style guide or that are negotiable. For example:

- Spelling, capitalization, and hyphenation of terms used in the project

- Acceptable jargon

- Abbreviations used, including in measurements

- Terms to use when referring to particular user-interface controls, such as field, drop-down list, pop-up list, slider

- Correct prepositions to use with various elements of the user interface—for example, do you do something "in" or "on" a window; is text typed "into" or "in" a field?

- Precise introductory wording for some help types

- Special requirements for this audience, such as:

  - Whether the use of "they" and "their" as singular pronouns is acceptable

  - Whether writers should use limited English—for example, if the application is to be translated into other languages

  - Any terms to be avoided, including non-English abbreviations or words, or terms that your audience might find confusing or unacceptable

Many companies adopt a commercially available style guide, and only note any additions or changes in the company or project style guide. Several style guides are listed in Appendix C, "For More Information."

Production editing online help

Production editing covers a range of issues and is generally done as the last step before final release of the help system to production. Most of these issues should have been detected and fixed earlier in the development cycle. For example, the help prototype stage should have included testing file conversions and graphic formats, and other display issues and solutions to major problems should have been found at that time.

At the production editing stage, you're looking for display and linking problems that have slipped through the other stages of editing. Copyediting or other checking of earlier drafts of the help should have found most of the problems discussed in this section, but last-minute changes sometimes have unexpected effects.

If you've been doing most of your editing on paper up to this point, then production editing—on screen—is vital. Many online display problems cannot be seen on a printout, and some things that look wrong on a printout actually display correctly on screen. Final layout (after content editing) may introduce problems.

For browser-based help, you may need to use a variety of screen resolutions, browsers, operating systems, and download speeds, to find all the problems. You won't need to check every topic under all conditions; a representative sample will find the majority of problems.

In addition to checking for display problems, you need to verify that:

- The final build includes all topics that should be there, and no topics that should not be there, especially if the project has used conditional text or more than one source file.

- All the errors found during copyediting have been corrected.

- Any notes from one team member to another have been removed.

Finding and fixing display problems

Online display problems usually come from three sources:

- File conversion to an online format from a word-processing or desktop publishing program, especially if the source document was originally designed for print output

- The way text and graphics are displayed on screen (often a platform-specific problem)

- Poor choices by the designer or writer

Most problems can be fixed, but some must be avoided by finding another way to present the information. This section looks at several common online display problems and accessibility issues.

Graphics

With graphics, what works well in print is usually not the same as what works best online. A full treatment of graphic formats, and how to prepare graphics that are optimized for your project's needs, is outside the scope of this book. See Appendix C, "For More Information," for some references.

If the writer or graphic artist didn't choose an appropriate format when creating or capturing graphics, it's probably too late to do anything about it at the production editing stage. Make a note to have clear specifications (and instructions on how to achieve them) written for the next release.

Here are some problems to look for:

- Graphics too large or too small
- Graphics not cropped to show only the relevant part
- Graphics inconsistent in size, resolution, or color
- Blurry graphics
- Jagged fonts in graphics
- Unnecessary graphics
  - Decorative rather than informative
  - Too many screen captures

Hotspots (links)

Hotspot is another term for *link*. Hotspots can be text, graphics, or part of a graphic or image map. Here are some common linking problems:

- **Poor choice of words.**
  If the link text is part of a sentence, be sure to choose words that establish the context, so the reader can get a good idea of what the link leads to. Don't make the words "click here" into a link, because screen readers for the blind will be unable to provide the context to the user.

- **Hotspots too close together in text or image maps.**
  In text, if adjacent words (for example, in a list) are separate links, the user may be unable to tell that they are not all part of one link, especially if the links are not underlined. For example:

  Popular pets are <u>cats</u>, <u>dogs</u>, <u>birds</u>, and <u>goldfish</u>.

  In graphics (image maps), if the hotspots do not correspond with discrete elements in the graphic, users may be unable to tell that more than one hotspot is present. (One way to overcome this is by using JavaScript to change the color of the hotspot when the mouse cursor is on it; this works well on maps, for example.)

- **Hotspots too large or too small.**
  In text, avoid hotspots that run over more than one line, or hotspots that are very short, perhaps only 1 or 2 characters long. In graphics, avoid hotspots that are only a few pixels in height or width. Many users have difficulty clicking on a small area, even if they can see it's there.

- **Hotspots not easy to distinguish from other text.**
  Don't get too creative with your text links. It's often best to leave them in the default color and style, which readers can usually change to suit their preferences; or add an icon that is used consistently throughout your help to indicate a link. The "Show Me" icon is an example.

  Because the default link indicator is usually green or blue with underlining, don't use underlining for emphasis or to indicate headings.

- **Too many colors.**
  Readers won't understand or remember a complex color scheme for links, and some people won't be able to distinguish the colors anyway, so there's no point in cluttering your files with irritating and confusing color differences within the text.

Tables

Some conversions to a help or Web format cause column or row alignment problems in tables, particularly when some cells straddle two or more columns or rows. The spacing and alignment of text within cells may also be converted incorrectly. This problem should have been tested much earlier, during the prototype stage, but you need to check now to make sure everything is correct.

Wide tables, particularly those converted from landscape pages, are often a problem in help files, because they require the reader to scroll horizontally. Row headings disappear off the left side of the screen when the reader scrolls to the right. Even worse, occasionally the rows in a wide table will wrap to the next line, making nonsense of all the columns. If possible, change the table to make it easier to read on screen, or define the first column (containing the row headings) to be in a non-scrolling region. Reconsider whether the table must be in the help, or if it can be divided into several smaller tables.

Long tables can be a problem because the column headings disappear off the top of the screen when the reader scrolls down. If possible, define the first row (containing the column headings) to be in a non-scrolling region, or break the table into several tables. Web-based help may load significantly faster if you break long tables into short ones, but beware that if you don't code carefully, sometimes this solution causes column widths to change, making the group of tables look inconsistent and messy.

Bullets and numbered lists

Problems with lists often arise during conversion of a document from a format such as Microsoft Word. For example, indentation may be inconsistent, numbering may not restart where it's supposed to, or numbering may restart when it's not supposed to.

Using carefully defined styles will usually solve these problems. For some hints, check some of the Web-based resources listed in Appendix C, "For More Information."

Indentation

Although the judicious use of white space is important in help files, just as it is in print, don't waste space on excessive indentation because it can quickly lead to very narrow columns of text in small help windows. If you're converting from a print-oriented document, careful definition and use of styles in the help should solve these problems.

Check the help for inconsistent indentation, which usually comes from writers applying the wrong paragraph styles or—worse—manually overriding styles.

Inconsistent help window sizes and placement

Older WinHelp files often suffered from the "fit window size to text" syndrome, where different types of windows would open in different sizes and appear in different places on the screen. I've seen this happen with Web pages, too. A reader following several links could be faced with help windows popping up apparently randomly on the screen, in different sizes (and often with different colored backgrounds or banners); many people find this irritating if not confusing.

The distinction between "main help windows" and "secondary help windows" is generally lost on users, so use the same size and placement for all windows. Define an appropriate window display size and placement and use it consistently. Enable scroll bars and window resizing, to allow users to customize the help.

Of course, some types of help—field help or glossary definitions, for example—require small pop-ups, placed next to the field they describe. Users expect this behavior, so it is not a problem.

Finding and fixing accessibility problems

Production editors need to consider the issues covered in "How will the help meet accessibility criteria?" in Chapter 3, "Developing Specifications." The major issues should have been tested and any problems fixed at the prototype or early draft stage. The production editor should verify that the help meets the specifications.

A full discussion of accessibility problems and how to avoid them would require another book. Some good books on this subject are listed in Appendix C, "For More Information."

Prioritizing changes

If you have limited time available for rewriting or fixing other problems found during editing, divide the necessary changes into three categories, and do them in order of priority:

1. Changes that must be made because the content is factually incorrect or the wording is unclear or ambiguous and may lead to serious misunderstanding, or changes that are required for legal reasons.

2. Changes that improve the writing or presentation but are not essential to understanding.

3. Changes that the vast majority of the audience won't care about or probably even notice—even if the editor considers them essential points of grammar.

Conclusion

This chapter summarizes general copyediting and production editing issues and focuses on special requirements for online help. A style guide is an important part of the specifications for any writing project. Online help must be checked on screen, even if it is also checked on paper.

Updates and corrections to this chapter can be found on Hentzenwerke's Web site, **www.hentzenwerke.com**. Click "Catalog" and navigate to the page for this book.

Chapter 11
Usability Testing on a Budget

If you avoid testing your help system for usability because you think it takes too long and costs too much, read this chapter to learn how to find 80 percent of problems quickly and inexpensively.

Software developers and their managers are generally aware of the need to test software for usability, but they often don't understand the value of testing user guides and online help for usability, or the difference between usability testing and other forms of testing. They may think it takes too long and costs too much to fit into the project's schedule and budget.

In fact, user documentation (including online help) needs to be usability tested as much as the software does. Such testing can be done quickly and inexpensively, and the consequences of not conducting early usability tests can be quite expensive. According to experts, 80 percent or more of usability problems are found with only four or five subjects. If found early, these problems can be fixed at little cost and without delaying release of the product or the help. If found at the end of the development cycle, usability problems can be quite expensive and time-consuming to fix.

A full discussion of usability testing would take another book; several good ones have been published. Excellent information is also available on the Web. Some resources are listed in Appendix C, "For More Information." Particularly relevant are two chapters in Steve Krug's *Don't Make Me Think* (2000), which describe how to conduct tests on a limited budget using inexperienced people, if that's your only choice—and why that's a better choice than not doing any usability testing at all.

What is usability?

Usability is "the extent to which a product can be used by specified users to achieve specified goals with effectiveness, efficiency, and satisfaction in a specified context of use." That's a somewhat ponderous way of saying a product is usable if people can use it quickly and easily to accomplish their goals.

For a help system, users' goals generally include finding required information, understanding the information, and applying the information to solving their immediate problems or answering their questions. Help-system usability includes these elements:

- Easy to learn—can people use the help system the first time they open it?

- Easy to remember—can people use the help system more easily the next time?

- Effective—can people easily navigate through the help system, understand the content, and put it to use to solve their problems?

- Efficient—can people find what they need in the help system and accomplish their goals in a reasonable amount of time?

- Satisfying—Do people have a good feeling about using the help system? Do they feel it was worth their time to use it? Will they use it again?

Usability is dependent on users' perceptions and experiences. A help system can pass objective tests for information included, links between that information, links from the product to the information, and so on, but if users' experiences are negative (for any of the reasons discussed in Chapters 5 through 9 of this book), then the help fails a usability test.

Usability testing, therefore, is a way to discover how users perceive and use the help system, by observing them actually using the help and then analyzing the data to diagnose problems and recommend changes.

 Usability is not the same thing as accessibility, although the two concepts are related. A help system or Web site is considered accessible if people with disabilities can use it as effectively as people without disabilities. Thus a help system could be quite accessible but very unusable, if everyone has difficulty understanding and using it.

Planning for usability testing

Most people think of usability testing as something that's done at the end of the project, during the system-testing phase of software development, when the help has been integrated with the software. Testing at that stage is certainly important and should be done, but you can also do a lot of valuable usability testing earlier in the help development cycle.

 Don't wait to test for usability until the end of the project—when it's too late to fix problems before the help system is released for production. Test at several stages during help development.

In the early stages of help development, usability testing overlaps considerably with reviewing and developmental editing. In later stages of help development, usability testing complements other forms of testing. See "What types of testing are required?" in Chapter 1, "Planning an Online Help Project."

What you call this work (reviewing, editing, testing) doesn't matter, as long as you consider important usability issues. These issues are covered in more detail in Chapters 5 through 10 of this book.

- Terminology
- Icons
- Design of the table of contents
- Design of the internal navigation scheme
- Design of the index
- Contents of topic types
- Writing style
- Use and presentation of lists, tables, and diagrams

 Don't skip usability testing just because you have no experience and can't afford to hire a usability expert to help you. Almost any testing is better than none, but you do need to plan a bit.

What to test when

Divide your usability testing into four stages, as summarized in **Table 1** and described in the following sections.

Table 1. What to test at each stage of help development.

Stage of help development	Items to be usability tested	Purpose of testing (questions you are trying to answer)
Planning	Task definition Terminology Icons	What should be in the specifications?
Prototyping	Overall design (fonts, colors, layout) Navigation within help system Draft table of contents Draft index design	Are the specifications suitable, or do they need improvement?
Early draft	Contents of topic types Writing style Use and presentation of lists, tables, and diagrams	Are writers producing material that meets the specifications? Are specifications suitable, or do they need improvement?
Production	All of the above General helpfulness	Did we get it right?

Usability testing during planning stage

At the planning stage, you are either developing specifications and a style guide for the help system of a new product or you are refining existing specifications for an upgrade from a previous version of the product.

You can include the testing described in this section during another stage of the project if you don't get a chance to do it during the planning stage.

Help for an upgraded product. If you're working on help for an upgrade to an existing product, some informal usability testing has already been done for you. You may have already modified the specifications to take into account any known problems. Gather any available information about problems in the existing help system—for example, calls to a help desk or questions sent to a users' group. You could also test the existing help in the same way as covered under "Usability testing during production editing stage" later in this chapter.

Help for a new product. If you're working on help for a new product, the planning stage is a good time to ask some representative users about terminology and icons you plan to use. If your draft table of contents is sufficiently developed, test it too at this stage; otherwise, do that during prototyping.

You may have already done much of this work when you were conducting your audience and task analysis, if you had the chance to observe or talk with real users. If, however, you had to rely on discussions with marketing people or software developers, it's a very good idea to test your decisions with real users. Although editors and subject-matter experts should be involved at this stage too, you may be surprised at the results you get from users.

Usability testing at this stage is usually done as a pen-and-paper exercise. One method uses index cards. Print one word, phrase, or icon on each card. Show the cards one at a time to users and ask what they think the words or icons mean, or what they think they would find if they clicked on the word or icon. Place a row of cards on a table and ask users which word or icon they would pick to do a particular task or find some specific information.

Use the results from this test to help you write the detailed specifications and the style guide for the help system.

Usability testing during prototyping stage

During prototyping, you may have several opportunities to ask users for their input regarding navigation and design issues. If terminology and icons weren't tested at an earlier stage, include them now.

Paper prototype. To usability test a paper prototype, print screen diagrams or mockups on landscape pages, so they look something like a computer screen. When a user chooses a link, show the printout of the topic that the link would lead to.

Electronic prototype. To usability test an electronic prototype, use a mockup or working prototype on a computer. If the links work, let test subjects click the links after telling you what they think they'll find.

Ask users what they would click on to learn more about the topic at a conceptual level ("What the heck is XX anyway and why would I want to use it? What are the consequences of choosing X or Y?") or at a more detailed level ("What format does this date need to be in? Is this field case-sensitive?").

Be careful not to ask leading questions—that is, questions that help test subjects figure out the answers. Ask questions like "What are you thinking? What information do you think you would want next? What do you think you should do now? What do you like about this page? What do you dislike about this page?"

Record users' reactions. Did they find what they expected after clicking a link? Did they understand what was going on? Did the terms and icons make sense to them? If you're including browse sequences, do users understand what to do to move through the sequence? Do they understand that there is a sequence?

Incorporate changes into your specifications. Changes might include modifications to topic content, not just design and navigation. If your client, manager, or software developers have been resisting authorizing the use of context-sensitive help or task-oriented help, feedback from this stage might provide the arguments you need to change this decision.

If for any reason you need to make major changes to your original help system design, conduct a second prototype test.

Usability testing during early draft stage

Your specifications look good, but do they work with users? You want to find out at the early draft stage, when only a few representative topics have been written. If you need to make major changes, now is the time to decide on them—not when the entire help system is written. At this time, you are testing:

- Contents of topic types
- Writing style
- Use and presentation of lists, tables, and diagrams

Show some representative topics to the test subjects and ask them questions. You might say, "You want to do X using the software, but you need help. When you click the Help button on the software, here is the help topic you will see. Please tell me what you think of this topic. Does it tell you what you would want to know? Is it too simple or too complicated? Easy or difficult to follow? Why? Are you not sure what some of the words mean? Which ones?"

At this point you're looking for users' reactions, not asking them to complete a task. Take notes on what they say, and also mark their reactions on a scale of 1–5 or Easy–Difficult or something similar (see "What are you going to measure?" later in this chapter).

Incorporate changes into your specifications and the writing of new topics, as well as changing the draft topics.

Usability testing during production editing stage

Here's where your test subjects get to work with the full help system, preferably integrated with the product. Did you get it right?

Usability testing of the help system at this stage is often done as part of usability testing of the software itself. If that's the way it's done in your organization, work with your QA group to ensure that the help is well tested. Perhaps you can contribute the test questions. As a last resort, do some additional testing yourself.

Testing at this stage is often more formal than some of the tests you conducted at earlier stages. Ask the test subjects to complete specific tasks. Some tasks might be entirely within the help system itself—for example, "Find out what part of the software you would use to do XX." If the help system has been integrated with the software, other tasks would involve doing something with the software that requires looking up some information in the help.

Conducting usability tests

If possible, be part of the overall product usability testing team, because many problems with the help turn out to be software bugs or problems with the user interface.

Here are the steps to follow when conducting a usability test:

1. Define testing objectives and methods.

2. Write test materials (scenarios for testers to follow).

3. Recruit participants.

4. Set up test environment.

5. Conduct the test.

6. Analyze and report on the results.

You can do all of this in three days: one day for steps 1–4, one and a half days to conduct the test (with three or four subjects), and half a day to analyze the results and prepare a report. You might need more test subjects and more time for a major product, but you are mainly looking for categories of problems, not every specific instance.

 Sample test plans, forms, and test materials are available on the Toolkit page of Society for Technical Communication's Usability Special Interest Group's Web site, http://www.stcsig.org/usability/resources/toolkit/toolkit.html.

Defining testing objectives and methods

Defining your objectives and methods is an important step that often gets overlooked by inexperienced (or rushed) testers.

- What are your goals for the test?

- Who is the audience?

- What are you going to measure?

- How will you collect the data?

What are your goals for the test?

Goals might vary at different stages of usability testing. Some typical goals include answers to the following questions:

- What are users' first impressions of the help system?

- What do users want to find in the help system?

- What are the trouble spots in the help system?

- Can people find what they want to know? How quickly?

- Is the level of detail correct—not too much or too little?

- Is any important information (from the users' point of view) missing?

- Is the information clear, unambiguous, easy to understand, and easy to put to use?

Usability testing is not specifically looking for accuracy of information or language problems, although incorrect information (if discovered) must be noted. Technical accuracy should be covered by technical reviews and language problems by copyediting.

Who is the audience?

Refer to the user profiles and personas you developed during early planning (see Chapter 2, "Analyzing Audiences and Tasks"). How many user types do you need to test? Specify characteristics for test subjects, to use when recruiting people.

Although it's a good idea to have your test subjects match the user profiles you're designing for, don't get too hung up on this aspect if you later can't find suitable people. You can learn valuable information from people who don't fit your user profiles.

What are you going to measure?

Measurements can be qualitative (subjective) or quantitative (can be measured or counted). Choose the measurements that are appropriate for the stage of testing, the audience, and your test goals.

Qualitative measurements are often on a scale of 1 to 5 or "Easy" to "Difficult" or "Completely satisfied" to "Totally unsatisfied," or they may be subjective comments recorded by the person conducting the test. If you use a scale, choose one that suits your needs, using terms that fit the question. In addition, make notes on test subjects' reactions and comments.

Examples of qualitative measurements and reactions include:

- Did the user find the task easy or difficult?

- Did the user think selected help topics (and the help system as a whole) included too much, not enough, or just the right amount of information?

- What are the user's concerns or problems?

- What are the user's expectations and desires?

Examples of quantitative measurements include:

- How long did it take the user to do the task?

- Did the user successfully complete the task on the first try (yes/no), or on another try (which one)?

- If the user was unable to complete a task—for example, locating information in the help system—was it because the information was missing, incorrect, or could not be found?

How will you collect the data?

Decide how you are going to collect the data. For example, the tester usually marks the responses rather than having the test subject fill out a questionnaire.

If you plan to use a video camera (recording what's happening on screen) or audio tape to record the session, don't rely on the tape as your only record of the session; take notes as well. Equipment can fail, and you might not have time to go over hours of tape afterwards. Use tapes to refresh your memory of what happened, if it's not clear from your notes.

During the test, ask subjects to tell you what they are thinking while they are doing a task. Take notes on their responses. After the test, ask a few planned questions and then let them talk freely about their experience, what they found easy or difficult, and any suggestions they might have for improvements.

You might have two people conducting the test—one taking subjective notes, and the other recording time taken to complete tasks, number of errors per task, and so on. One person can do both jobs, but it's often easier for two people to share the work.

Writing test materials (scenarios for testers to follow)

There's an art as well as a science to writing good test scenarios. If possible, get an experienced usability tester to write them for you, but don't let a lack of experience stop you from conducting the test. Almost any testing is better than none, unless you deliberately try to skew the results to get the answers you want, instead of those you need.

It's important to have a script to follow when conducting tests, so you ask each subject the same questions and you don't lead them to the answers you want.

When testing at early stages, your questions may not relate to specific tasks, either in the software or the help. You're looking for general problems with terminology, icons, navigation, and organization. At later stages, questions should relate more closely to user tasks.

Base your test materials on task lists. You may be able to reuse the user scenarios you developed when planning the help system, or you may need to develop new scenarios.

Choose a few tasks that require subjects to find obscure information or make use of advanced features, so the subjects need to consult the online help to complete a task. This approach helps you find usability problems with the online help, not the software itself. If you usability test the help at the same time as the software, you may want to sometimes suggest that subjects look in the help (but don't say where or how) and other times leave subjects to decide for themselves whether to use the help when struggling with a difficult task.

You could vary your task questions with the knowledge and experience level of the test subject, but if you do that, be sure to test several subjects for each group of task questions.

When possible, have the test materials edited and reviewed, to make sure they focus on significant tasks and are of a suitable level of difficulty.

Examples of test tasks

Figure 1 shows some sample tasks for a usability test of a software product (adapted from Jonathan Price and Henry Korman, *How to Communicate Technical Information*, 1993, page 341). Two of the three tasks explicitly involve using the help system.

---

1. Using the Contacts database, look up the California phone number of a business called Cozbiz, with offices in California, New York, France, and Japan. Write the California number here. _____

2. Locate all the contacts in Canada, and print out a list showing their names, addresses, and phone numbers, sorted by postal code. You may want to look in the online help about finding information, sorting, and printing.

3. Find out what the command Match (on the Utilities menu) can do for you, using the Glossary and Index of the help. Write the answer here.
   _____

Figure 1. Sample tasks for a usability test.

Recruiting test subjects

A good sample of typical users is best. Five people should be enough. A "typical user" depends on your product. What personas did you develop? Find people like them, either among your existing customer base or (if appropriate) among students or members of the public who may be willing to act as test subjects.

If you have the budget, you could get a recruiter or temp agency to find the test subjects for you. Be sure the agency understands your needs; some agencies specialize in providing test subjects, but others may have no idea what you're talking about. Your company's HR department may be able to help, or you may need to find the test subjects yourself.

If you can't get representative users, at least find someone in another part of your company who is not familiar with the product but has some of the characteristics of your audience. Be sure that staff members understand they are not being "graded" on their performance—that the idea is to find problems with the help system, not with the people using it.

Outside test subjects should be paid for their time and out-of-pocket expenses. Staff members should at least get a mug of tea or coffee and a snack.

Set up a schedule with plenty of time between tests for you to write up your notes, get the room and the software ready for the next person, and discuss initial impressions with other members of the team.

Setting up the test environment

You don't need special equipment, just a room with a table or desk, two chairs, a computer (if this isn't a pen-and-paper test), and an Internet connection if necessary. If you can use a video camera to record the session, do so. If possible, set the camera up with a cable to a monitor in a nearby room, so other people can observe the test without disturbing the subject.

Although usability experts say to conduct tests in a quiet, uninterrupted environment, consider doing some testing in users' real environments using the same equipment they use. For example, are typical users working in a noisy "cube farm" or factory floor, in bad lighting conditions, or being constantly interrupted? Do they have small or badly lit monitors such as those on some laptops or handheld machines?

Conducting the test

If at all possible, choose a calm, patient person to conduct the tests. This person's main job is to observe, take notes, put the test subjects at ease and encourage them to talk, without leading them to the "right" answers.

The facilitator does not need to be part of your team. Perhaps someone from your company's training or HR departments could fill this role. Don't let lack of a suitable tester stop you from conducting the test.

More about the role of the tester (also known as a *facilitator*) is given in the books on usability testing. Steve Krug (*Don't Make Me Think*, 2000) has a particularly good summary.

Analyzing and reporting on the results

Immediately after conducting each test, write down any observations you didn't have time to record during the test (or expand on cryptic notes so you'll be able to understand what they mean later). When all of the test subjects are done, summarize your observations in a list or table.

Go over the results and write down your conclusions, which may be in general terms like "xxx needs more work," then decide what needs to be done about each identified problem and assign a priority to each change. You don't need to write an elaborate document complete with statistical analysis—a simple table can be quite sufficient.

If you're working with a team of writers, or some changes might need agreement from the software developers, organize a meeting to discuss your findings and decide what to do.

Prioritizing problems and making changes

Classify the usability problems by severity level (see **Table 2**, adapted from JoAnn Hackos, *Managing Your Documentation Projects*, 1994).

Table 2. *Severity levels of documentation problems.*

Severity level	Description
Life-threatening	Problem may cause someone to be injured or killed.
Major	Problem may cause a loss of data or a mistake that results in lost work. User's work flow is severely disrupted. Legal requirements are not met.
Minor	Problem may cause a minor interruption of the user's work flow.
Annoyance	Problem may cause customer to perceive a lack of quality standards in your organization, but causes no harm, lasting or temporary.

As with editorial changes, if you have limited time available for fixing problems found during usability testing, divide the problems into three categories and fix them in order of priority. Don't simply fix the easy ones first—they are usually the most trivial.

1. Changes that must be made because content is factually incorrect, unclear, or ambiguous and may lead to serious misunderstanding (severity levels 1 and 2).

2. Changes that improve the writing or presentation but are not essential to understanding (severity levels 3 and 4).

3. Changes that the vast majority of the audience won't care about or probably even notice, especially if test subjects' reactions or opinions are contradictory (severity level 4).

Conclusion

Any usability testing is better than none. Do it early and often. A small number of test subjects will generally find 80 percent of the problems. If resources are limited, fix the problems in order of their severity, not in order of the ease of fixing them.

Updates and corrections to this chapter can be found on Hentzenwerke's Web site, **www.hentzenwerke.com**. Click "Catalog" and navigate to the page for this book.

Appendix A
Sample Plans and Specifications

Get going quickly with these sample plans and specifications. Fill in the blanks in the files on the Web site.

This appendix provides a sample online help plan and sample help specifications for the TreeLine software product, which was mentioned in earlier chapters of this book. Use these examples as guidelines when writing your own plan and specifications with the help of the templates you can download from the Web site.

The examples show the kind of information that goes into these documents. All projects are different, so yours may require quite different decisions. Refer to Chapter 1, "Planning an Online Help Project," and Chapter 3, "Developing Specifications," for more information.

Other excellent sources of information on plans and specifications are Hackos (*Managing Your Documentation Projects*, 1994), the CD included with Deaton and Zubak (*Designing Windows 95 Help,* 1996), and Dodge and Ward (*Planning and Designing Multi-Authored Help Systems*, 1999). See Appendix C, "For More Information," for full details on these publications.

Templates

You can download templates for an online help plan, high-level specifications, and detailed specifications from the Hentzenwerke Web site.

Online help plan: helpplantemplate.rtf.
High-level specifications: highlevelspecstemplate.rtf.
Detailed specificatons: detailedspecstemplate.rtf.

Example 1: Online help plan for TreeLine

This online help plan is for the TreeLine software product.

Purpose of project and product

TreeLine is an open-source information storage program. It could be called an Outliner or a Personal Information Manager (PIM). It stores almost any kind of information. TreeLine uses a tree structure that makes it easy for users to keep things organized. The output can be shown on the screen, printed, or exported to HTML.

The existing online help is in a single Readme file and is also available as a database within the product itself.

The purpose of this help project is to provide context-sensitive online help at the dialog level, written in language suitable for the target audience.

Audience
The audience for this product has the following characteristics.

- Users could be any age and from any background, but they probably have had some experience with PIMs or at least are familiar with the concept, even if they've never used one themselves.

- They may have used a PIM at school or work, but not on their personal computers.

- If Linux users, they are more comfortable with a graphical user interface (GUI), not a command-line interface. (Windows users are GUI users by definition.)

- They're probably using TreeLine because they want to, rather than being told by their boss that they have to.

- They're probably using the program on a desktop or laptop computer in a home environment, rather than walking around a factory floor or other "field" situation, where a handheld or palmtop machine (which runs its own PIM software) would be more suitable.

- They might have older hardware or software and want a program that doesn't use a lot of memory or processing power.

- They might have a dial-up connection to the Internet, but no connection is required except for downloading the program.

Personas
The following personas describe two typical users of the TreeLine program.

Tim A. is a 57-year-old freelance journalist. He has stacks of handwritten notes on ideas for articles and research supporting those ideas: Web sites, e-mail and newsgroup postings, pages in books, and contact names and phone numbers. He also has photocopies and printouts of material, as well as files saved on his computer. He tries to keep the paper organized in manila folders and ring binders, but some things are relevant to more than one topic, so cross-referencing them is a problem, and keeping track of the hard copies and the computer files gets confusing. Tim hates wasting time chasing down all the information he wants for an article when he needs it; he knows he's got it there somewhere, but it's hard to find.

Tim has a broadband Internet connection and an older desktop computer with somewhat out-of-date software (Microsoft Windows 98 and Office 97) that serves his needs quite well. He knows how to use e-mail, a browser, a word processor, and other tools of his trade, but he doesn't know much about their technical aspects and is completely uninterested in learning. If he has a problem with the hardware or software, he calls his son or a friend for help. Tim doesn't want to upgrade his software or install new programs, because he doesn't want to spend time learning how to use them. On the other hand, he wants to organize his notes better, so he's willing to try something new, as long as it's easy to use and the help or manual tells him exactly what to do; he doesn't want to have to figure it out for himself.

Emma B. is a 22-year-old university student. Her parents can't help her financially, so she's on a tight budget. Most of her research is done on the university's machines, but she has a secondhand laptop running Linux and other open-source software, for personal use and for essay writing at home. Her needs for organizing a lot of information are similar to Tim's, but her attitude toward software is very different. Emma hates the "hand-holding" type of online help that tells her the steps to follow (which she usually considers obvious) but doesn't answer her real questions. She's used to working with databases, she likes to know what's going on behind the scenes with the software she uses, and she likes to be able to customize her experience as much as possible.

User task analysis

Typical users' tasks (after installation of the program) are as follows.

- Enter information by typing
- Enter information by importing from another source
- Organize information into "nodes"
- Move information from one node to another
- Copy information from one node to another
- Edit information or nodes
- Delete information or nodes
- Format information (for example, numbers, date, time, text, true/false)
- Find information in the database by using various selection criteria or filters
- Sort retrieved information
- Print retrieved information
- Export retrieved information in various forms, including text and HTML

Competitors, previous software, or integrated systems

Any members of the audience who have used outliners or PIMs before may expect to be able to do similar things with this one, so the help should answer the types of questions they might have. Other members of the audience will not have used similar products, so they may be completely unfamiliar with any of the concepts.

TreeLine help does not need to be compatible with any other help systems, because the program is not integrated with an office suite or other software.

This version of TreeLine is a minor upgrade from previous versions. The help system, however, will be a major upgrade in terms of both functionality and content.

Help development process

One person (the technical writer) will be responsible for planning the project, writing specifications, prototyping, and writing the help. The software developer will review the help. The writer and the developer will both test the help.

Because this is an existing product with a functional help system, and major changes to the software user interface are not expected in the next software release, the timing of help development is not required to fit in with the timing of software development.

Reviews, edits, and tests

- Three reviews are required, as described later in this plan.
  1. When the help plan, specifications, and prototype are complete
  2. When the table of contents is complete, and the writing and indexing are 20 percent complete
  3. When the help project is complete
- One copyedit is required at the final draft stage, as described later in this plan.
- Two tests are required, as described later in this plan.
  1. At the prototype stage
  2. When the help is complete

First review

The first review will be conducted by the software developer, who is responsible for:

- Approving the plan, specifications, and prototype
- Authorizing the work to continue to the next review

Entry criteria for the review: Plan and specifications to be provided in PDF format. Prototype to be provided in electronic format as intended for final product, to include at least one sample topic of each type to be included in the final help, showing typical links between them, and a working draft of the table of contents.

Exit criteria: Work to date approved by developer, after any necessary rework by writer.

Second review

The second review will be conducted by the software developer, who is responsible for:

- Approving the table of contents and the style and content of the sample topics
- Finding any factual errors in the content
- Authorizing the work to continue to the next review

Entry criteria for the review: Complete table of contents and 20 percent of the topics to be provided in electronic format as agreed upon at the prototype stage.

Exit criteria: Work to date approved by developer, after any necessary rework by writer.

Third review

The third review will be conducted by the software developer, who is responsible for:

- Finding errors and omissions in the final content and index

- Approving the help system for integration with the software product

Entry criteria for the review: All topics, table of contents, and index are complete.
Exit criteria: Work approved by developer, after any necessary rework by writer.

Copyedit

Copyediting will be done by a suitably qualified editor, using the guidelines provided in the style guide and specifications for the project.

Copyediting will be done as the help topics are written, with a final production edit when all topics, table of contents, and index are complete.

First test

The technical writer will test the electronic prototype of the help, to ensure that the help displays as designed, and that the internal navigation aids work as intended.

Second test

The technical writer will test the final version of the help, to ensure that the help displays as designed, the internal navigation aids work as intended, and the correct help topic is displayed when the user requests help.

The developer will test the final version of the help, to ensure that the links from the product dialogs to the help work.

Assumptions, dependencies, risks

To ensure that the help system is ready when the next version of the software is to be released, the technical writer must have access to working software at the beta or earlier stages of development.

The software developer must be available to review and test the help at the specified times. The developer must immediately inform the writer of any changes to the software when those changes are implemented.

Help-development step	Dependencies
High-level help specifications	High-level software design specifications
Detailed help specifications	Detailed software design specifications
Detailed task analysis High-level prototype	Functional specs, high-level design specs, detailed task list
Detailed prototype Outline and map Write, index, edit	Detailed software design specs
Technical reviews	Reviewers available
Test the help	Working software, help integrated with software
Release the help	Help integrated with software

Schedule

The schedule for help development is as follows, assuming all dependencies are met.

Help-development step	Approximate start date	Approximate end date
High-level help specifications	3 May 2004	6 May 2004
Detailed help specifications	7 May 2004	12 May 2004
Detailed task analysis	13 May 2004	19 May 2004
High-level prototype	20 May 2004	28 May 2004
Detailed prototype	1 June 2004	8 June 2004
Outline and map	9 June 2004	15 June 2004
Write, index, edit	16 June 2004	2 July 2004
Technical reviews	6 July 2004	9 July 2004
Test the help	12 July 2004	16 July 2004
Release the help	19 July 2004	—

Contingency plans

If the dependencies are not met, or the writer is unable to complete the work on time because of illness or other circumstances over which she has no control, the help system may be delivered later. In that case, the existing help text, written by the developer, will be shipped with this release of the product, and the new help system will be verified and shipped with the next release of the product.

Related documents

Related documents within this project are as follows.

Document	Person responsible
High-level help specifications	Technical writer
Detailed help specifications	Technical writer
Project style guide	Technical editor
Use cases	Developer
User scenarios	Developer
User task list and task map	Developer and writer
Test plans	Developer and writer

Example 2: High-level specifications for TreeLine help

These specifications are for the TreeLine software product.

Related user documentation

The online help will be the only user documentation for the product.

Type of help to be provided

Help will be provided as a set of HTML files that can be displayed in any browser.

Interactions between help and application

Help will be connected at the dialog level. Field-level help will be provided from the dialog-level topics, not directly from the application.

Users will be able to access the help from a Help item on the menu bar of the main window, Help buttons on major dialogs, and by pressing the F1 key. This requirement requires some programming changes to the existing product, to enable dialog-level connections.

Media types to be used

Help will include text and static graphics (including image maps), but no animated graphics, video, or audio content.

Tools for writing, editing, indexing

The help-authoring tool to be used is HelpScribble, which can produce a table of contents and index as well as the help topics. The help source files (in RTF format) are compatible with other help-authoring tools, so future upgrades are not dependent on the tool used this time.

Screen captures will be made using PrintScreen and processed in Microsoft Paint. Any other graphics will be produced using Paint Shop Pro. Graphics will be saved in PNG format.

Topic types required

The following topic types are required:

- Overview—what you can do and which parts of the application to use for what task

- Procedural ("how to")—detailed steps to accomplish tasks

- Dialog-level—include field descriptions

- Problem-solving—diagnostics and solutions

Presentation of help windows

Because the help will be displayed in the user's default browser, the size, shape, and position of the browser window will be determined by the user, not preset by the writer.

The help will be provided as a frameset, with the table of contents and index in the left-hand pane. For browsers that don't support frames, the table of contents and index will also be available as topics.

Navigation aids

In addition to the table of contents and index, navigation within the help system will be provided by "Related Topics" links.

Accessibility criteria

Use CSS (cascading style sheets), not inline styles. Do not use fixed font sizes; define larger or smaller fonts as percentages of the base font, and leave the base font size to be set by the user's browser. Ensure that the user will be able to access the help by a mouse click or by pressing the F1 key. Ensure high contrast for all users, including color-blind users, by using black text on a white background.

Example 3: Detailed specifications for TreeLine help

These sample specifications are for the TreeLine software product. The choices made here probably won't apply to your project. Replace them with relevant choices.

Primary sources

Use the following documents as primary sources of specifications:

- *Read Me First! A Style Guide for the Computer Industry*, 2nd edition, Sun Technical Publications, 2003

- *Chicago Manual of Style*, 15th edition, University of Chicago Press, 2003

- Webster's New International English Dictionary

Writing conventions

If not otherwise specified, use the writing conventions described in *Read Me First! A Style Guide for the Computer Industry*, 2nd edition, by Sun Technical Publications, 2003.

- Use short, simple, easy-to-understand words and sentences.

- Avoid the passive voice.

- In general, use the present tense.

- Use strong subject-verb constructions. Avoid weak constructions such as "There are."

- Be concise; avoid wordy phrases.

- Use gender-neutral language.

- Use sentence-style capitalization for headings.

- Capitalize and spell screen element names to match their appearance on the screen. To avoid ambiguity, capitalize the first letter of each word (including articles, prepositions, and so forth) in the names of menus, dialog options, commands, fields, and other such elements.

- Use American, not British spelling; consult the preferred dictionaries.

- Use metric units of measurement.

- Spell out numbers from one to ten unless they are used as units of measure or examples of data. Use numerals for zero and for numbers 11 and greater.

- Capitalize the first word of each item in a list.

Terminology

Use the terminology conventions and preferences described in *Read Me First! A Style Guide for the Computer Industry*, 2nd edition, by Sun Technical Publications, 2003.

Abbreviations and acronyms

Short form	Long form
HTML	HyperText Markup Language
PIM	Personal Information Manager
URL	Uniform Resource Locator, also known as a "Web address"

Design and layout

Follow these specifications.

Colors

Background	White
Topic title	Dark blue
Body text	Black
Table heading background	White
Table heading text	Dark blue
Table background	White
Table text	Black

Layout of topics

All titles and text flush left.
First paragraph: no indent.
Following paragraphs: first line indent 0.8 cm.
No space between paragraphs.
Space after titles 6 pt.
[Other layout specifications omitted]

Graphics

Capture screens using a standard Windows color scheme.
Crop screen captures to show only the relevant portions.
Save graphics as PNG files.
Embed graphics in help file.
[Other details omitted]

Table of Contents

[Details omitted]

Index

[Details omitted]

Content of topic types

This section describes the topic types to be used, their purpose, their contents, and how they are accessed from the application.

Overview topics

Overview topics provide a brief description of the application's purpose and intended use. They may be presented as a single topic (if brief) or as a sequence of related topics.

Users access overview topics through the index, contents page, or links from procedural and other topics. Overview topics cover such issues as:

- Purpose of the application

- Description of changes and new features that will affect users and their work

- Guidance on where users can get help or application support

- How the user can get started with the application (for example, a brief description of the navigation options)

- How the user can get help on the application

- Brief description of the most common or important tasks a user can perform, with links to procedural topics

- Brief description of user roles, if any

Overview topics contain:

- Topic title

- Description or discussion, using bullet points where appropriate

- Links to related topics

Sample overview topic 1

<table>
<tr><td>Title of help topic</td><td>**Welcome to TreeLine Help**</td></tr>
<tr><td>Brief description of process or purpose</td><td>This help file has two parts, the "how to" section and the reference section. The "how to" section contains step-by-step instructions for how to accomplish certain things with TreeLine. It does not explain everything you could possibly do with TreeLine, but clearly explains basic tasks so you can get up to speed quickly.

The reference section includes a screen-by-screen description of the program and a detailed explanation of the program's functions.

The two parts are cross-referenced, so you can move easily between the "how to" explanations and the reference material.</td></tr>
<tr><td>Links to related information</td><td>**How to use TreeLine**

A tour of the TreeLine main window
Starting a new TreeLine document
Adding information to a TreeLine document
Getting information out of a TreeLine document

Reference

Formatting and Node Types
Field Types
File Import and Export
Output
Tree Data Manipulation</td></tr>
</table>

Sample overview topic 2

Title of help topic	**A tour of the TreeLine main window**
Brief description of process or purpose	TreeLine's window is divided into two panes: • The view on the left shows the entire tree structure. • The view on the right shows various information about the tree node that is selected in the left pane. The right pane is tabbed to show one of three different views of the data: • The "Data Output" view shows the formatted text for each node and is read-only. • The "Data Editor" view shows a text edit box for each data field within a node. • The "Title List" view shows a list of node titles that can be modified using typical text editor methods.
Links to procedural help	**Related topics**
Links to related information	<u>Changing the view</u> <u>Using menu and toolbar commands</u> <u>Starting a new TreeLine document</u> <u>Adding information to a TreeLine document</u> <u>Editing information in a TreeLine document</u>

Procedural ("how to") topics

Procedural topics provide step-by-step instructions on how to complete a user task. User tasks often involve the use of more than one window or dialog box.

Users access procedural topics through the index, contents page, or links from window- or dialog-level topics. Procedural topics contain:

- Task title (briefly identifies and describes the task procedure)

  - Phrased using terms that are familiar to users; users should be able to predict whether the topic matches their task goals just by reading the title.

  - Begins with the gerund form of a verb (ending in –ing; for example, Submitting), followed by an object.

- Purpose of task or procedure from the user's perspective (a sentence or two that explains the task purpose, its usefulness, and the expected outcome or result)

  - Explains, in the users' own language, why they would want to perform this task and how it relates to their work; focuses on user needs, not on how the application works

  - Answers questions like "What user problem does the procedure solve?" and "How does the procedure fit into the user's work?"

- Prerequisite conditions or tasks that users must perform before beginning this task

  - If the prerequisite tasks have procedures of their own, link to help topics for those tasks.

- Step-by-step instructions or procedures (numbered steps that describe how to complete the task)

  - Begins with an infinitive tag—a short phrase beginning with "To"; for example, "To submit the form:", "To change an emergency contact:". The infinitive explains the purpose of the steps that follow.

  - Each step describes a single action, such as clicking a button, selecting an item, choosing a menu item, or typing text in a field. It is written as a verb followed by a noun phrase.

  - If there are multiple ways to complete an action, document a single approach and choose the approach that users will easily understand and learn. Provide cross-references to other topics that describe alternative ways to complete the action, but don't provide cross-references for common actions.

  - Procedural topics typically contain about 5 or 6 steps. If a procedure starts to exceed 8 steps, consider breaking it into two procedural topics.

- What happens now? What happens after a user performs the task steps (outcome; results and follow up information)?

- Related Topics list

Sample procedural topic

Title of help topic	**Adding information to a TreeLine document**
Purpose	To add information to a TreeLine document:

Steps	1. Click Edit > Add Child on the menu bar.
	    A text input box (showing the word "New") appears in the
	    left-hand pane.
	2. Type a title for this node. (You can change it later.)
	3. Click on the Data Editor tab in the right-hand pane.
	4. Type the information to be included in this node.

What happens now?	The title (heading) of the node appears in the left-hand pane. To add subheadings, create additional "child nodes" under this node. You can now rearrange the order of nodes, add nodes, format the information, manipulate the information in a variety of ways, and output the information.
Related topics	**Related topics** What is a node? Editing information in a TreeLine document Formatting information in a TreeLine document Outputting information from a TreeLine document

Dialog-level topics

Dialog-level topics provide information on how to use the active window or dialog, a description of tasks that can be accomplished with the dialog, and details on dialog elements and processing.

Dialog-level topics are displayed when the user presses F1 or a Help button on an application window or dialog. In some cases dialog-level help will be combined with procedural help—for example, when a brief description is sufficient.

Dialog-level help topics contain:

- Window or dialog title

- Brief overview of what the user can do in the window. When writing the overview:

  - Focus the description on why users would want to use the dialog and how it will help them complete their work.

  - Keep the explanation brief, because dialog-level help is meant to be a memory jogger rather than a tutorial. If a longer explanation is necessary, link to a conceptual topic.

- ▪ Do not describe anything beyond the current application window unless this window must be used in a specific sequence and you need to refer to other windows as a result.

- ▪ Describe what the user can do in the specific parts of the dialog, if the interrelationship between the components of the dialog would not be obvious from the field-level or procedural help for the dialog.

- Procedures for the tasks a user can perform with the window or links to such procedures

- Descriptions of fields, buttons, and other controls

Sample dialog-level help topic

Title of help topic	**Configure Data Types dialog**
Brief description of what the user can do	Use this dialog to define the characteristics of different data types within TreeLine. Data types can include headings, ordinary text, dates, pictures, and others.
How to use this dialog (may include field descriptions or links to procedural help)	Select a predefined data type from the Data Type list. You can then format the selected data type using the other fields and controls on this dialog. To add a data type to the list, click the Modify List button.
	Fields and controls

	Title Format
	    [Describe field]
	Output Format
	    [Describe field]
	Modify List button
	    Opens a dialog for adding, renaming, or deleting data types.
	Field Type button
	    Opens a dialog for formating the selected field.

Links to related information	**Related topics** Adding, deleting, and renaming data types Formatting fields

Field-level topics

Field-level topics cover both fields and controls (buttons and check boxes). These topics should answer the question, "What is this and why would I want to use it?" For entry fields, these topics also answer the question, "What do I type here and what restrictions are there on how I enter the information?"

In TreeLine help, field-level descriptions are not separate topics; instead, they are included in procedural and other topics. When writing field-level descriptions for TreeLine:

- Use a "definition list" style, as shown in the examples.

- Be brief, and include only essential information.

- For an entry field, include a brief description of the information that should be typed into the field, if it is not obvious.

- If relevant, mention any restrictions such as case sensitivity, limits on numbers of characters, or the format of dates.

- If relevant, include information about why a setting might be disabled and how the user can enable it.

Sample field-level topics

> **Field Type**
> A variety of field types are provided with TreeLine. You cannot define new field types or delete the ones provided, but you can modify the output format of the supplied field types. Choose a field type from the list in this box.

> **Format Help button**
> Several field types have a choice of predefined output formats. When you choose one of these field types, the Format Help button becomes active. Click the Format Help button to display and choose from a list of formats available for the selected field type.

Problem-solving topics

Problem-solving topics provide lists of common problems with the software, and include procedures and recommendations for diagnosing and solving the problems.

Users access problem-solving topics from the index, contents page, or links from other topics, including error message topics.

These topics contain:

- Topic title (a statement of the problem)

- Diagnostics list or matrix, if required, with links to solutions (may be part of one topic, or separate topics)

- Solution to problem, if it can be provided in one topic

Sample problem-solving topic

Title of help topic	**Error loading XML Parser**
Diagnostics	This error message typically means that TreeLine could not find a necessary XML library.
Solution, or (in complex cases) links to solution topics	Under Linux, Python uses external libraries for parsing. Installing either the expat library or the PyXML package should fix the problem.
	Under Windows, Python includes a parser, so this error should not be seen unless files are missing or corrupt.

Conclusion

This appendix includes examples of an online help plan, high-level specifications, and detailed specifications. Although the specifics in the examples are unlikely to apply to your product, you should be able to adapt the examples for your own use. The Web site for this book includes templates for the same documents.

Updates and corrections to this chapter can be found on Hentzenwerke's Web site, **www.hentzenwerke.com**. Click "Catalog" and navigate to the page for this book.

Appendix B
Help Types and Tools

This appendix provides a summary of some common types of help, their pros and cons, and the tools you can use to produce them. It covers Windows, Macintosh, and Linux environments.

Before choosing help development tools, decide which type of help you need for your project, and whether you intend to use a single source to produce material for both printed and online formats. Then choose tools to help you create that type of help.

 You do not need to create a help system on the same operating system on which it will be used. For example, many people use a Windows-based help-authoring system to create help to be viewed on other operating systems.

Help types and development tools change frequently. This list was correct in June 2004. Inclusion of a tool on this list is not an endorsement or recommendation of the tool. This list is not complete; other help types and tools exist. A good source of information about help systems and tools is Char James-Tanney's Helpstuff, **http://www.helpstuff.com/**.

Types of help

On Windows systems
The main types of help for Windows are provided, not surprisingly, by Microsoft. In addition, other forms of HTML-based help—particularly those displayed in a Web browser—also run on Windows.

HTML Help
This is Microsoft's HTML-based help. It creates a compiled file, which is displayed in a viewer that requires components of Internet Explorer to be installed on the user's computer. The standard help window has three panes, but the display can be modified by the help author and partially controlled by the user. The compiled file (CHM) is in a compressed form. Tools exist to display CHM files on other operating systems.

WinHelp
This is Microsoft's older help format. The basic WinHelp window has only one pane, but help authors can produce pop-up and secondary windows. For a non-standard format, such as tri-pane, you must supply an extra DLL with the help. The major help-authoring tools simplify the process of creating non-standard formats.

Longhorn Help—on its way

The next generation of Microsoft help formats is scheduled to ship with the next version of Windows (code-named "Longhorn") in 2005 or later. Previews of the format are available on the Microsoft Web site and from commentators such as Char James-Tanney and Matthew Ellison, who describes Longhorn as "a Help system designed specifically for creating task-based assistance that can be highly integrated with the application UI."

On multiple platforms using a Web browser

Almost any browser-based HTML system can be adapted to work as a help file for non-browser-based programs as well as for Web applications and other browser-based programs. These help systems can usually work on Windows, Macintosh, Linux, and other operating systems.

The major help-authoring tools produce browser-based help systems under a variety of names. These help systems can include capabilities such as dynamic tables of contents, multi-level indexes, full-text search, context-sensitive help, related-topics controls, expanding text, and more.

JavaHelp

Sun Microsystems' help platform for Java applets and applications is designed for cross-platform compatibility and easy integration with Java applications. It requires the Java Runtime Environment (JRE), which includes the JavaHelp viewer. Help-authoring tools can create the JavaHelp three-pane window format with a content pane, a navigation pane, and a navigation toolbar. The navigation pane includes a collapsible table of contents, a keyword index, full-text search, and custom tabs.

On Apple Macintosh systems

Macintosh operating systems prior to OS X used a variety of help types and systems. Help for programs on OS X is generally HTML-based (or XML-based) and displayed in the built-in Help Viewer.

On Linux systems

Older Linux programs generally provided plain-text help files of a type known as "Man pages" in Unix. More recent programs, particularly those aimed at a wider audience, are HTML-based (or XML-based) and often displayed in a browser. For Java applications, you can use JavaHelp.

Tools

Help types and development tools change frequently. This list was correct in June 2004, but it is far from complete. I have listed tools that are often mentioned by technical writers, plus a few others that I'm familiar with. Many other help-authoring tools exist. A good list is provided on **http://www.helpstuff.com/vendor.html** by Char James-Tanney.

Help-authoring tools running on Windows

Microsoft Help Workshop

You can produce fully functional WinHelp by using the free Microsoft Help Workshop. Look on your hard disk or the Windows CD for a file named HCW.EXE.

HTML Help Workshop

You can produce fully functional HTML Help using Microsoft's free HTML Help Workshop. To download the latest version from the Microsoft site, go to

http://msdn.microsoft.com/library/default.asp?url=/library/ en-us/htmlhelp/html/vsconHH1Start.asp

Third-party help-authoring tools can make the job easier, and provide features not available in the basic help workshops. I've listed just a few of the many tools. Most have evaluation copies available, and most can produce a variety of help output formats—and a printed manual—from a single file. Some tools require Microsoft Word; others work with Adobe FrameMaker; some stand alone.

Tool	Vendor's Web site
Author-It	http://www.author-it.com/
Doc-to-Help	http://www.componentone.com/
EasyHelp/Web	http://www.eonsolutions.co.uk/
HDK	http://www.vmtech.com/
Help & Manual	http://www.ec-software.com
HelpBreeze	http://www.solutionsoft.com/hlpbrz.htm
HelpScribble	http://www.helpscribble.com
QuickHelp for Windows	http://www.excelsoftware.com
RoboHelp and related products	http://www.ehelp.com/
West Wind HTML Help Builder	http://www.west-wind.com/
WebWorks Publisher	http://www.quadralay.com/
Mif2Go	http://www.omsys.com/
Deva Tools for Dreamweaver	http://www.devahelp.com

Other tools running on Windows

These are just a few of the many tools available as add-ons to help-authoring tools or for capturing screens and general graphics manipulation.

Tool	Vendor's Web site	Function
HTML Indexer	http://www.html-indexer.com/	Creates back-of-the-book style indexes for Web sites and other HTML documents.
FAR	http://www.helpware.net/	Utilities for manipulating HTML files in conjunction with the HTML Help Workshop. Includes search-and-replace across multiple files and directories.
Adobe Photoshop	http://www.adobe.com/	High-end graphics manipulation tool.
Adobe Photoshop Elements	http://www.adobe.com/	Graphics manipulation sufficient for most help-authoring requirements.
Paint Shop Pro	http://www.jasc.com/	Does most graphics creation and editing tasks. Includes screen-capture capability.
Fullshot	http://www.fullshot.com/	Captures Windows screens. Many features.
SnagIt	http://www.techsmith.com/	Captures Windows screens. Many features.
GIMP	http://www.gimp.org/	Open-source, full-featured graphics package. Includes screen-capture capability.

Tools running on Macintosh operating systems

Some Macintosh help systems are produced using help-authoring tools running on Windows. Help authors also produce HTML-based Macintosh help systems by using any available Macintosh-based HTML editor.

One Macintosh-based help-authoring system is QuickHelp for Macintosh, from **http://www.excelsoftware.com/**.

Many excellent graphics programs are available for the Macintosh. For more information, please consult Web sites or printed publications devoted to the Macintosh.

The open-source, full-featured graphics package GIMP is available for the Macintosh as well as for other systems. **http://www.gimp.org/**. The GIMP includes screen-capture capability.

Linux

Changes are rapid in the Linux development world, so by the time you read this, other help types and authoring tools may be available. For more information, please consult Web sites or printed publications devoted to the Linux platform.

Some HTML-based Linux help systems are produced using help-authoring tools running on Windows. Help authors also produce HTML-based Linux help by using any available Linux-based HTML editor.

The most complete documentation tool available for Linux (and other systems) is DocBook, a general-purpose XML and SGML document type definition. Authors use various text-processing software to produce structure markup in DocBook files and export them to formats such as HTML. For more information, see **http://www.docbook.org/**.

One Linux-based help-authoring system is QuickHelp for Linux, from **http://www.excelsoftware.com/**.

The open-source, full-featured graphics package GIMP is available for Linux as well as for other systems. **http://www.gimp.org/**. The GIMP includes screen-capture capability.

> Updates and corrections to this chapter can be found on Hentzenwerke's Web site, **www.hentzenwerke.com**. Click "Catalog" and navigate to the page for this book.

Appendix C
For More Information

This appendix lists some books and Web pages with more details on topics covered in this book. Web sites and their addresses change frequently, often without warning or redirection to their new location. This list was correct in June 2004.

General references

Boggan, Scott, David Farkas, and Joe Welinske, *Developing Online Help for Windows 95*, International Thomson Publishing, 1996, ISBN 1850322112. Reprinted by Solutions, Inc, 1999, ISBN 0967064201. Both editions are out of print; secondhand copies may be available.

> Contains excellent information on writing online help, most of which is applicable to any form of help. Topics include the documentation set, the design process, general issues related to writing help, writing procedural and other help topics, performance support help (wizards and coaches), creating the index, and others.

Deaton, Mary and Cheryl Lockett Zubak, *Designing Windows 95 Help*, Que, 1996, ISBN 0789703629. Out of print; secondhand copies may be available.

> Focuses on the design aspects of WinHelp development. Chapters cover audience, window handling, navigation, graphics, multimedia, context-sensitive help, case studies, and more. Part III (nearly 300 pages), titled "Designing a useable system," covers planning a help system, designing and organizing content, designing the interface, designing navigation to the user's advantage, and others. An excellent resource, if you can find a copy.

Hackos, JoAnn and Dawn Stevens, *Standards for Online Communication*, John Wiley & Sons, 1997, ISBN 0471156957.

> Covers Web pages and other online documentation as well as help systems: defining the process, analyzing users' information needs, structuring the system, designing the interface, providing navigation aids, writing topics, and more. Includes a CD-ROM containing a WinHelp file of the book, designed according to the principles taught in the book.

Horton, William K., *Designing and Writing Online Documentation: Hypermedia for Self-supporting Products*, John Wiley & Sons, 1994, ISBN 0471306355.

> One of the classic books about online documentation, this book does not go out of date; the principles discussed and guidelines provided are applicable to any online situation. Covers much the same material as Hackos' and Stevens' *Standards for Online Communication*.

Price, Jonathan and Henry Korman, *How to Communicate Technical Information: A Handbook of Software and Hardware Documentation*, Benjamin/Cummings, 1993, ISBN 0805368299.

> Although this book doesn't specifically discuss online help, it's an excellent introduction to user-centered technical writing. It was written at a time when task-oriented documentation was a new concept, not yet commonly adopted.

Schriver, Karen, *Dynamics in Document Design*, John Wiley & Sons, 1994, ISBN 0471306363.

> Discusses how people read and create documents. Provides a close look at readers as they try to make sense of the documents typically found at home, at work, or at school. Includes numerous examples and case studies to assist writers and designers in creating usable documents.

TECHWR-L, the Technical Writers' List, **http://www.raycomm.com/techwhirl/**.

> General discussions about technical writing and related topics. To join, send an e-mail message to <lyris@lists.raycomm.com>. Type "**sub techwr-1 Your Name**" in the body of the message, and leave the subject line blank.

Accessibility

King, Andrew B., *Speed Up Your Site*, New Riders, 2003, ISBN 0735713243.

> Covers the optimization of almost everything that goes into a Web page: HTML, XHTML, CSS, JavaScript, graphics, multimedia, compression, keywords, and more. Much of this is relevant to online help systems, particularly those delivered over the Web.

Slatin, John M. and Sharron Rush, *Maximum Accessibility: Making Your Web Site More Usable for Everyone*, Addison-Wesley, 2003, ISBN 0201774224.

> A practical book, with examples and explanations, many of which are also relevant to online help systems.

Society for Technical Communication, AccessAbility SIG (Special Interest Group), **http://www.stcsig.org/sn/**.

> Includes introductory information and lists of resources on accessibility. You may be surprised at the range of disabilities and other factors that you should consider.

Thatcher, Jim, *et al.*, *Constructing Accessible Web Sites*, Glasshaus, 2002, ISBN 1904151000.

> Explains accessibility guidelines and how to achieve them, with practical, real-world examples. Much of this material is relevant to online help.

Web Accessibility Initiative (WAI), **http://www.w3.org/WAI**.

> Includes "Getting Started: Making a Web Site Accessible,"
> **http://www.w3.org/WAI/gettingstarted**.

> A detailed discussion of guidelines that page authors should follow in order to make their pages more accessible for people with disabilities as well as more useful to other users, new page-viewing technologies (mobile and voice), and electronic agents such as indexing robots.

Web Design Group, **http://www.htmlhelp.com/**.

> Promotes the creation of non-browser-specific, non-resolution-specific, creative and informative sites that are accessible to all users worldwide. Offers material and tools on a wide range of HTML-related topics, Web authoring frequently asked questions and frequently encountered problems, style guide, standards for HTML authoring, a guide to accessibility, image tips, a handy list of RGB color codes, and links to related sites.

Audience analysis and personas

Hart, Geoff, "Prescriptive Audience Analysis: Moving Beyond the Purely Descriptive," **http://www.raycomm.com/techwhirl/magazine/writing/prescriptiveanalysis.html**.

> Describes the prescriptive approach to audience analysis and its applications for technical writers, including the differences between stereotypes and personas.

Goodwin, Kim, "Perfecting Your Personas," **http://www.cooper.com/newsletters/2001_07/perfecting_your_personas.htm**.

> A good introduction to the art of developing personas during audience analysis.

Hackos, JoAnn and Janice C. Redish, *User and Task Analysis for Interface Design*, John Wiley & Sons, 1998, ISBN 0471178314.

> Covers in detail every step of the task-analysis process and discusses the methodologies behind it, including what observations to make, questions to ask, and questions to avoid; how to turn the information you've gathered into design ideas; how to create paper prototypes of your design; and how to conduct usability tests with your prototypes to find out if you're on the right track.

Graphics

Brierley, Sean, "Screen Captures 102," **http://www.raycomm.com/techwhirl/pdfs/Screen_Captures_102.pdf**.

> Provides extensive hands-on information about screen captures.

Graphics on the Web, **http://www.w3.org/Graphics/**.

> A good introduction to the use of graphics on the Web.

Horton, William K., *Illustrating Computer Documentation: The Art of Presenting Information Graphically on Paper and Online*, John Wiley & Sons, 1991, ISBN 0471538450.

> A classic book in the industry, as relevant now as when it was written. Excellent for technical writers and editors who are not trained technical illustrators; it provides clear principles and guidelines with examples.

Ray, Eric J., "Understanding Graphic File Formats," **http://www.raycomm.com/techwhirl/magazine/technical/graphicfileformats.html**.

> A brief reminder of what the various kinds of graphic formats are and how to use each of them when they're the most appropriate—not merely most convenient—for the situation.

WebReference pages on optimizing Web graphics, **http://www.webreference.com/dev/graphics/index.html**.

> A good introduction to graphics formats and optimizing graphics for online use. Includes pages on tools, tips, and techniques, and references to other sources of information.

Weinmann, Lynda, *Designing Web Graphics.4: How to Prepare Images and Media for the Web*, 4th edition, New Riders, 2002, ISBN 0735710791.

> Everything you need to know about designing and creating graphics for online display. Even if the sections on inserting graphics into Web pages aren't relevant to your help project, the conceptual and practical information about file formats, color calibration, small file sizes, and other details are valuable.

Help types and tools

Becker, Joseph's HelpMaster site **http://www.helpmaster.com/**.

> A large selection of WinHelp, HTML Help, and HTML-related files and hints, with pointers to tools or copies of them on the site.

Cline, Dana, **http://www.logicsmith.com/**.

> Contains information and papers on various aspects of help authoring, software development, and other related fields. The Forums area contains interactive discussion forums for WinHelp, HTML Help, and the Software Development Pub.

HATT (Help Authoring Tools and Techniques).

> An Internet mailing list for online help authors to share information about online help tools and techniques. To subscribe, send a blank e-mail message to <HATT-subscribe@yahoogroups.com> or go to this Web page: **http://groups.yahoogroups.com/group/HATT**.

James-Tanney, Char, **http://www.helpstuff.com/**.

> Includes articles about various help authoring issues, help types, tips for writing help, comparisons of tools, and more.

JavaHelp, **http://java.sun.com/products/javahelp/**.

> Background information on JavaHelp. You can download software and a user's guide.

JavaHelp-interest, a public mailing list on JavaHelp.

> To subscribe, send an e-mail message to <listserv@javasoft.com>. Type "**subscribe javahelp-interest**" in the body of the message, and leave the subject line blank.

> To view the archives, go to **http://archives.java.sun.com/archives/javahelp-interest.html**.

Knopf, David, **http://www.knopf.com/**.

> Tips, tricks, shortcuts, and workarounds. Good, brief summaries of major online help formats with key resources, recommended readings, and pointers to discussion lists.

Microsoft's HTML Help, **http://msdn.microsoft.com/library/default.asp?url=/library/ en-us/htmlhelp/html/vsconhh1start.asp**.

> A good starting page for information on HTML help.

Indexing

Bonura, Larry S., *The Art of Indexing*, John Wiley & Sons, 1994, ISBN 0471014494.

> A thorough, practical handbook for technical writers. Clearly presents effective indexing techniques applicable to both print and online materials.

Mulvaney, Nancy C., *Indexing Books*, University of Chicago Press, 1994, ISBN 0226550141.

> An in-depth discussion of the analysis and editorial judgment calls involved in indexing. Builds on various style guides, especially the *Chicago Manual of Style*'s extensive chapter on indexing. The principles apply equally to indexing online materials.

Planning and specifications

See also books in the General References section.

Dodge, Kelly A. and Lauren P. Ward, "Planning and Designing Multi-Authored Help Systems," 1999, **http://logicsmith.com/files/kdodge.zip**.

> Contains excellent examples of specifications.

EPSS Central, **http://www.epss.com/**.

> Information on analysis and design of software systems that result in improved business performance (Electronic Performance Support Systems [EPSS], Performance Centered Design, Knowledge Management), and Performance Support Engineering. Site includes key concepts and "how to do it" information as well as resources (books, articles, conferences, tools).

Hackos, JoAnn, *Managing Your Documentation Projects*, John Wiley & Sons, 1994, ISBN 0471590991.

> Detailed discussion of project planning for documentation managers, technical writers, editors, consultants, and anyone called upon to produce high-quality technical documentation (printed or online) on time and within budget. Includes guidelines, real-life case studies and scenarios, templates, checklists, forms, and more.

Use Case Zone, **http://www.pols.co.uk/use-case-zone/index.html**.

> Provides links and information on use cases. Includes slides of a tutorial, "The Art of Writing Use Cases," by Rebecca Wirfs-Brock.

Usability

Barnum, Carol M., *Usability Testing and Research*, Addison-Wesley Longman, 2001, ISBN 0205315194.

> A leading textbook on usability, aimed primarily at people who are new to usability and usability testing. Includes many examples of planning, conducting, and reporting usability tests.

Dumas, Joseph S. and Janice C. Redish, *A Practical Guide to Usability Testing*, Intellect, 1999, ISBN 1841500208.

> Filled with examples, the book discusses all the steps for planning and conducting a usability test, analyzing data, and using the results to improve both products and processes. Included are forms that can be used or modified to conduct a usability test.

Krug, Steve, *Don't Make Me Think: A Common Sense Approach to Web Usability*, Que, 2000, ISBN 0789723107.

> A great book, full of before-and-after examples and analysis. Includes two chapters on inexpensive usability testing and some sample test scripts.

Nielsen, Jakob, **http://www.useit.com/**.

> Nielsen is one of the leading Web interface usability gurus. His site includes many useful tips and guidelines.

Nielsen, Jakob, *Designing Web Usability: The Practice of Simplicity*, New Riders Publishing, 1999, ISBN 156205810X.

> Pulls together material from Nielsen's Web site into book form.

Quesenbery, Whitney, **http://www.WQusability.com/**.

> This usability expert's Web site includes downloadable copies of some of her published articles.

Rubin, Jeffrey, *Handbook of Usability Testing: How to Plan, Design, and Conduct Effective Tests*, John Wiley & Sons, 1994, ISBN 0471594032.

> A classic book on usability testing. Provides beginners with a full complement of proven templates, models, tables, test plans, and other tools and techniques. Includes real-life examples and case histories taken from a wide range of industries.

Society for Technical Communication, Usability SIG (Special Interest Group), **http://www.stcsig.org/usability/**.

> Includes introductory information and lists of resources on usability. The Toolkit page contains sample forms, plans, and test scripts that you can download. **http://www.stcsig.org/usability/resources/toolkit/toolkit.html**.

Writing, style, and copyediting

Chicago Manual of Style, 15th edition, University of Chicago Press, 2003, ISBN 0226104036.

> One of the most-used style manuals in the technical writing industry.

Copyediting-L, the copyeditors' discussion list.

> Discussions include substantive and technical editing as well as copyediting. To subscribe, send mail to <copyediting-L@listserv.indiana.edu> with the message "subscribe your name".
>
> Archives are available at **http://listserv.indiana.edu/archives/copyediting-l.html**.

Hart, Geoff, "The Style Guide is 'Dead': Long Live the Dynamic Style Guide," **http://www.raycomm.com/techwhirl/magazine/writing/dynamicstyleguide.html**.

> Argues that traditional style guides are too static for most writers, and don't take advantage of computer technology to make the writer's working life easier. Advocates making the guide dynamic through the use of templates, shortcuts, and other work aids.

Microsoft Manual of Style for Technical Publications, Third Edition, Microsoft Press, 2004, ISBN 0735617465.

> Covers terminology related to the Windows interface and its use, as well as general aspects of Microsoft style.

Nadziejka, David E., "Levels of Technical Editing," Council of Biology Editors, 1999, ISBN 0914340158.

> Proposes a new system of editing that considers the special nature of technical documents and the unique responsibilities of those who edit them. Argues that the primary editorial focus must be to help ensure that the technical content is complete, accurate, and understandable to the intended audience.

Rude, Carolyn, *Technical Editing*, 3rd edition, Longman, 2001, ISBN 020533556X.

> The leading text for courses in technical editing. Packed with examples and exercises to develop the principles and guidelines presented. The author emphasizes editorial responsibility at all stages of document development. Contains a chapter specific to online help and other online materials, and most of the practical editing material is applicable to both print and online.

Sun Technical Publications, *Read Me First! A Style Guide for the Computer Industry*, 2nd edition, Prentice Hall, 2003, ISBN 0131428993.

> Includes grammar and punctuation guidelines, typographic conventions, pointers on creating a bibliography (including how to reference online source materials), and guidance on indexing and graphic design; checklists and forms for editing, tracking manuscripts, and verifying production status; and tables of abbreviations, acronyms, and units of measurement. An excellent resource.

Troffer, Alysson, "Editing online documents, strategies and tips," 1999, in the online journal *Contentious*, **http://www.contentious.com/articles/V2/2-4/feature2-4a.html** and linked pages.

> An excellent summary; I wish I'd written it first.

van Buren, Robert and Mary Ann Buehler, *The Levels of Edit*, 2nd edition, Jet Propulsion Laboratory, Pasadena, CA, January 1980, JPL Publication 80-1, 26 pp. This paper is out of print, but a PDF copy is available at the following site: **http://www.io.com/~tcm/etwr2371/planners/levels_of_edit.pdf**.

> A classic paper on editorial tasks, grouping them into types and levels. Useful when negotiating with clients about the exact nature of an editor's duties.

Weber, Jean Hollis, "Developing a Departmental Style Guide," **http://www.raycomm.com/techwhirl/magazine/writing/styleguide.html**.

> Provides information that will help you in planning and developing a style guide.

Weber, Jean Hollis, "Escape from the Grammar Trap," **http://www.raycomm.com/techwhirl/magazine/writing/grammartrap.html**.

> Describes how to distinguish between essential and nonessential rules of grammar, punctuation, and usage.

Weber, Jean Hollis, "Working with a Technical Editor," .
http://www.raycomm.com/techwhirl/magazine/writing/technicaleditor.html.

> Looks at some aspects of the writer-editor relationship and what each can do to get the best results out of working together.

Updates and corrections to this chapter can be found on Hentzenwerke's Web site, **www.hentzenwerke.com**. Click "Catalog" and navigate to the page for this book.

Appendix D
Glossary

This appendix includes online help and computing terms used in this book.

The definitions in this glossary are adapted from several sources, including the *Microsoft Press Computer Dictionary*, Third Edition, 1998; FOLDOC, the Free On-Line Dictionary of Computing (**http://www.foldoc.org/**), various other dictionaries reached from the search engine Onelook (**http://www.onelook.com/**), and several of the books listed in Appendix C, "For More Information."

accessibility. The extent to which people with disabilities can use a help system, Web site, or other software as effectively as people without disabilities.

beta. A software product ready to release for outside testing.

bookmark. 1. In general Internet usage, a saved reference in the form of a URL or link to a particular location, page, or site. Called a Favorite in Microsoft Internet Explorer. 2. In WinHelp, a saved link to a particular topic in a help file.

browser (also called Web browser). An application that enables a user to view HTML documents on the World Wide Web, on another network, or on the user's computer; follow the hyperlinks among them; and transfer files. In addition, most current browsers can display graphics and video files, play audio files, and permit users to send and receive e-mail and to read and respond to newsgroups. Online help is increasingly being displayed in a browser.

browse sequence. The order in which writers link a series of topics together so readers can move easily from one topic to the next or previous topic in the sequence. In a help file, a browse sequence might be used to link a series of related topics, which are a subset of the help file; the file might contain numerous browse sequences. In a book-like file, such as an online user guide, the browse sequence could be the same as the order of topics in the contents list and could include every topic in the file. Readers could then move through the sequence of topics much like turning the pages of a book.

CHM. The file extension given to a compiled and compressed HTML Help file.

coach. Coaches help users work through complex, multi-dialog procedures and other situations that do not fit well into a single help topic. They give users instruction on one step of a procedure; users then perform this step in the application itself. If they need help with the next step, users can click a button on the coach window to go to the next page of instructions.

compiled help. One or more files that function as a working help system, with working links. May or may not be connected to the application it documents. Contrast with the source file, which may be in Word, RTF, text, or other format.

compress. To modify a file (using a special program) to save storage space or transmission time. The resulting compressed file is significantly smaller than the source file. Compressed files are often called "zipped."

conceptual topic. A brief description of the application's purpose, intended use, and most common or important tasks; fundamental concepts, components, or actions in an application; the theory, logic, or reasoning behind a task.

context IDs or **context numbers.** Numeric values assigned by programmers to elements of the user interface and associated with help topic IDs, to display specific help topics from individual dialogs, fields, or other controls in the program.

context-sensitive. Help topics relevant to the user's location in the application. This term is used to mean either dialog-level help or field-level help. Both types can be provided for the same application.

dialog (also called **dialog box**). In a graphical user interface, a special window displayed by the system or application to request a response from the user. These windows usually cannot be resized by the user and do not include a menu bar or toolbar.

edit. 1 a: to prepare for publication or public presentation; b: to assemble (as a moving picture or tape recording) by cutting and rearranging; c: to alter, adapt, or refine, especially to bring about conformity to a standard or to suit a particular purpose; 2: to direct the publication of.

editor. 1: someone who edits, especially as an occupation; 2: a device used in editing motion-picture film or magnetic tape; 3: a computer program that permits the user to create or modify data (as text or graphics) especially on a display screen.

embedded help. Provides the information that users need without their having to ask for it. It may be a pane that displays help alongside the application window; simple (or detailed) instructions shown on dialog boxes; tooltips, mouseovers, or other small messages at the bottom of an application window; or help that pops up on top of the application window and offers suggestions on how to do a task.

error message help topic. Provides help for the system messages that appear on the application's user interface. Describes what's happening, how to respond, and the consequences of the user's choices. If possible, the message itself should provide enough information so this type of help isn't required. However, if the choices are complex, message help may be required.

EPSS (Electronic Performance Support System). Software that provides job-related help to people while they're doing the job; for example, how to process a customer's order. EPSS is different from the online help for an application program, which tells people how to use the program itself, although EPSS may be integrated with an online help system. Some of the "wizards" in modern software are a form of EPSS, but many EPS systems are specific to an organization or an industry.

expert user. A person familiar with the application. Usually experts are also familiar with the platform and computer use in general. The term may be used to describe expert computer users who are not familiar with the application, but whose information-gathering needs are different from the needs of novices. A related concept is the "domain expert," a person who is very knowledgeable about the subject matter—for example, accounting—but is unfamiliar with the application.

FAQ (Frequently Asked Question) topic. Provides answers to common questions that users may have when working with the application.

favorite. See *bookmark*.

field-level topic. Sometimes called "What's this?" help: a brief explanation about a part of the interface (individual fields and controls within a window). See also *context-sensitive*.

GIF (Graphics Interchange Format). A graphics file format used for transmitting images on the Internet. Compare *JPEG, PNG, TIFF*.

glossary topic. Brief explanations of terms provided as pop-ups. Glossary terms may also be gathered into a single topic, organized alphabetically, that can be browsed.

help-authoring tool. Software that assists writers to prepare, maintain, track, compile, and test online help. Most forms of help can be written without using these products, but many people find the work easier with them.

Help menu. An item provided on the menu bar of application windows. Help menu items often include Contents, Index, and About, but may also have numerous other choices including Tutorial, Tip of the Day, and links to other documents or Web sites.

history list. In WinHelp and Web browser, shows the last several topics or Web pages that a user viewed.

hotspot. A section of text or graphic that, when clicked, takes the user to another topic. The term is generally used to refer to graphic links.

HTML (HyperText Markup Language). The markup language used for documents on the World Wide Web. HTML uses tags to mark elements, such as text and graphics, in a document to indicate how Web browsers should display these elements to the user and should respond to user actions such as activation of a link by means of a key press or mouse click.

HTML-based help. Help that uses HTML files, but is not specific to the Microsoft Internet Explorer environment. The term includes a range of help types, including those that are used with Web-based applications.

HTML Help. Microsoft's HTML-based help.

hyperlink. A connection between an element in a hypertext document, such as a word, phrase, symbol, or image, and a different element in the document, another hypertext document, a file, or a script. The user activates the link by clicking on the linked element. Also called *link, hot link, hypertext link*.

hypertext. Text linked together in a complex, non-sequential web of associations in which the user can move through related topics.

icon. A graphical representation of (a) an object on the user interface, such as a folder, document, or program; (b) a graphic symbol on a button or a clickable link.

Internet. The worldwide collection of networks that provide e-mail, the World Wide Web, and other services.

intranet. A communications network based on the same technology as the Internet, but available only to certain people, such as those within a company.

JPEG (Joint Photographic Experts Group). A standard for storing images in compressed form; often used on Web pages. A graphic stored as a file in the JPEG format has the file extension JPG. See also *GIF, PNG, TIFF*.

jump. A section of text or graphic that, when clicked, takes the user to another topic. Also known as *hotspot* or *link*.

link. See *jump*.

Lookup topic. Contains the codes, values, variables, parameters, or other data needed when filling in a report, making a calculation, or quoting a price.

navigation. Includes all the ways for readers to move around in a help file and find the information they want; for example, contents page, index, search function, browse sequences, cross-references and other links, and icons.

novice user. A person unfamiliar with your application, who may or may not be familiar with the platform or with computer use in general.

online help. Information that meets three criteria: Users can access it directly from the software interface (including browser-based interfaces and Web pages) by selecting an item on a help menu, by clicking a link or button on the interface, or by pressing a key (such as F1 or Help) on the keyboard; it provides guidance and assistance as users complete real work tasks, not just practice tasks, as found in tutorials; it usually provides an immediate answer to a question on a specific window or dialog.

overview topic. Contains extended narrative discussions with no explicit procedures (numbered steps). Intended to provide high-level information about the application as a whole, its functional areas and structure, or a narrower set of concepts related to a specific procedure.

page. 1. On the Web, a collection of files that display as one entity; may include text, graphics, sound, and video. 2. In a dialog box, one of several tabbed sections, only one of which is visible at a time.

palette. 1. In graphics programs, a collection of drawing tools, such as patterns, colors, brush shapes, and different line widths, from which the user can choose. 2. A subset of all the possible colors that establishes which colors can be displayed on the screen at a particular time.

PDF (Portable Document Format). The file format for Adobe Acrobat. PDF represents documents in a manner that is independent of the original application software, hardware, and operating system used to create those documents. A PDF file can describe documents containing any combination of text, graphics, and images in a device-independent and resolution-independent format.

persona. A fictional person who has the characteristics described in a *user profile*.

PNG (Portable Network Graphics). A file format for bitmapped graphic images, designed to be a replacement for the GIF format. See also *GIF, JPEG, TIFF*.

pop-up. A special kind of topic that appears in a window without buttons or title bar. A pop-up appears over the previous topic, and goes away at the next mouse click or key press. Normally used for definitions, dialog box control explanations, or "What's This?" topics.

problem-solving topic. Describes a common problem with the software, and provides procedures and recommendations for diagnosing and solving the problem. Also known as a *troubleshooting topic*.

procedure topic. Step-by-step instructions (usually numbered) on how to complete a task, with a minimum of explanatory narrative text. The purpose is to show how the application works and how to complete user-defined tasks. Often called directly from a dialog.

prototype help system. A draft help system, demonstrating the elements, topic types, links, and other features to be included in the working system. Early prototypes can be on paper; later ones should be working, although they may not contain specific information. Help authors often develop a prototype help system at the same time as the application prototype.

reference topic. Can contain narrative text but, unlike overviews, is intended to provide specific and discrete information that requires little or no conceptual explanation. May contain definitions, error messages, shortcuts, sample dialogs, and other topic types. Explains details beyond the "how to" level, such as command structure and options, keyboard shortcuts, and so on. Usually non-procedural. Generally aimed at more expert users.

review. To evaluate material for technical accuracy and completeness; correct the material as needed. Usually done by software developers or other subject-matter experts. Compare with *edit* and *test*.

SGML (Standard Generalized Markup Language). An information management standard adopted by the International Organization for Standardization (ISO) in 1986 as a means of providing platform- and application-independent documents that retain formatting, indexing, and linked information. SGML provides a mechanism for users to define the structure of their documents and the tags they will use to denote the structure in individual documents.

show-me topics. Demonstrate an action rather than merely describing it; for example, finding the location of an item on a submenu. Can be animated or static.

task analysis. Analyzing users' work and the tasks they perform, to determine how the software supports these tasks and what questions the help needs to answer.

task map. Lists the subtasks that relate to an overall task, and points to the topics that provide instructions for completing those tasks. Should include a brief description and list any prerequisite tasks and follow-up tasks. May cross-reference related tasks.

task oriented. Documentation, including online help, that provides how-to and other information from the point of view of users and their tasks, instead of describing how the system works.

test. To check software and online help to ensure that it works as specified, including internal and external links. In addition, usability testing checks for users' problems with the interface. Internal link testing is often called *reliability testing*.

TIFF (Tagged Image File Format). A standard file format commonly used for scanning, storage, and interchange of graphic images. Compare *GIF*, *JPEG*, *PNG*.

Tip of the Day topic. Brief hints and tips on how to use the software, usually provided so a new tip appears each time the program is started.

topic. The basic element of help files. A topic appears in a window, such as the main window, a secondary window, or a pop-up. It is equivalent to a printed page, but is generally shorter.

topic ID. An alphanumeric identifier assigned by a writer or authoring tool to a help topic. Used to specify the topic associated with a text or graphic link, or (when mapped to a context ID) the topic called by the application. In a Web application, the HTML file name may be used as the topic ID.

troubleshooting topic. Describes a common problem with the software, and provides procedures and recommendations for diagnosing and solving the problem. Also known as a *problem-solving topic*.

tutorial. Provides an environment in which users can practice procedures or experiment with data and results, without worrying about messing up their real data.

usability. The extent to which a product can be used by specified users to achieve specified goals with effectiveness, efficiency, and satisfaction in a specified context of use.

use case. A specific, behaviorally related sequence of transactions describing a way of using an application. A high-level description, often focused on what the system is doing. See also *user scenario*.

user. Any individual who uses a computer, regardless of their level of expertise, or amount of time spent using a computer.

user profile. A list of characteristics of a typical user in a specific category of users. See also *persona*.

user scenario. Developed from use cases, scenarios are detailed examples of the specific steps a user must perform to accomplish tasks, rather than generic descriptions. See also *use case*.

Web. Short for World Wide Web. One of the services available on the Internet. Web pages are displayed in a browser, and may include text, graphics, sound, and video.

Web browser. See *browser*.

window. The main, rectangular area in which application elements are displayed in graphical user interfaces. Usually contains a menu bar, one or more toolbars, a status bar, scroll bars, and other elements. Can often be resized by the user. Contrast with *dialog*.

WinHelp. Microsoft's older help format for Windows platforms.

wizard. Steps users through a series of actions and choices to help them accomplish a complex task. The data entered and choices made by the user when using the wizard are real application tasks and affect real data; they are not samples or demonstrations,

XHTML (eXtensible HyperText Markup Language). A reformulation of HTML 4.01 in XML.

XML (eXtensible Markup Language). A structured markup language derived from SGML. Now the standard for much Web site development, single-sourcing projects, and other documentation.

zip. See *compress*.

Updates and corrections to this chapter can be found on Hentzenwerke's Web site, **www.hentzenwerke.com**. Click "Catalog" and navigate to the page for this book.

Appendix E
Checklists

This appendix contains reminders of what you need to do at each step of the help planning and development cycle.

These checklists are available for download from the Hentzenwerke Web site. The file is titled checklists.rtf.

Planning the help project

Refer to Chapter 1, "Planning an Online Help Project," for details.

❑ Produce the help plan, which includes:

    ❑ Product analysis

    ❑ Audience analysis (see separate checklist for details)

    ❑ Competitive analysis

    ❑ Help aims and objectives

    ❑ Constraints on the help deliverables

    ❑ Assumptions

    ❑ Dependencies

    ❑ Risks

    ❑ Required tools and training

    ❑ Estimates (for each phase and key task and deliverable)

    ❑ Required resources

    ❑ Schedule, showing major milestones and interactions with development schedule

    ❑ Procedures and criteria for reviewing and testing the help

    ❑ Who does what editing, reviewing, and testing, and when

    ❑ Methods for editing and reviewing

    ❑ References to the help specifications

❑ Get stakeholders (client, software developers, marketing, others) to review and approve the plan.

❑ Periodically revisit the plan to assess the assumptions, dependencies, and risks, to provide input for any required schedule adjustments.

Analyzing audiences and tasks

Refer to Chapter 2, "Analyzing Audiences and Tasks," for details.

- ❏ Perform audience analysis.
    - ❏ Demographics
    - ❏ Experience
    - ❏ Roles
    - ❏ Attitudes
    - ❏ Other factors
- ❏ Develop personas.
- ❏ Perform task analysis.
    - ❏ Use cases and user scenarios
    - ❏ Lists of user tasks
    - ❏ User/task matrix
    - ❏ Flow diagrams
- ❏ Map help topics to task list.
- ❏ Develop list of typical audience questions.

Developing specifications

Refer to Chapter 3, "Developing Specifications," and Appendix A, "Sample Plans and Specifications," for details.

- ❏ Produce the high-level help specifications, which include:
    - ❏ Relationship between online help and other user documents
    - ❏ Type of help to be used
    - ❏ Connection to the application (field-level, dialog-level, embedded, other)
    - ❏ Procedures and criteria for working with programmers
    - ❏ Help testing and error-correction procedures and criteria
    - ❏ Media types required
    - ❏ Information types and levels required
    - ❏ Topic types required
    - ❏ Presentation of help windows or pages
    - ❏ Navigation aids to be used
    - ❏ Accessibility criteria

- ❑ Produce the detailed help specifications, which include:
    - ❑ Reference materials
    - ❑ Design and layout
    - ❑ Help navigation scheme
    - ❑ Content of topic types
    - ❑ Task matrix
- ❑ Begin creating the project style guide.
- ❑ Get stakeholders to review and approve the specifications.

Developing a prototype

Refer to Chapter 4, "Prototyping the Help System," for details.

- ❑ Produce the help prototype.
    - ❑ Design and navigation
    - ❑ Sample topics
    - ❑ Working navigation and other links
    - ❑ Outline and map of help system
    - ❑ Browse sequences
- ❑ Get stakeholders to review and approve the specifications.
- ❑ Test the prototype for usability.
- ❑ Review prototype as required.

Developing the table of contents

Refer to Chapter 6, "Producing the Table of Contents and Index," for details.

- ❑ Using the table of contents, can you find answers to sample questions from your task and question list?
- ❑ Is the flow of information logical from the readers' point of view?
- ❑ Are the topic titles (headings) informative? Are they task-oriented?
- ❑ Are the headings parallel in structure?
- ❑ Is the table of contents grouped by information type (for example, overviews, procedures, reference)?
- ❑ Is the presentation consistent?

If the answer to any of the following questions is "yes," you need to make changes to the text of the document or the entries in the table of contents.

- ❑ Is information missing?
- ❑ Is the table of contents too detailed or not detailed enough?
- ❑ Are the headings too long or too short?
- ❑ Do any entries jump to the wrong help topic?

Developing the index

Refer to Chapter 6, "Producing the Table of Contents and Index," for details.

- ❑ Using the index, can you find answers to sample questions from your task and question list?
- ❑ When you do some random lookups in the help, is the term or topic in the index?
- ❑ Is the first word of each index entry meaningful (something the reader is likely to be looking for)?
- ❑ Do all topics have a main entry, not just a subentry? (They might also have a subentry.)
- ❑ Does every topic (except pop-ups) have at least one meaningful index entry?
- ❑ Do all keywords jump to the correct help topics?

If the answer to any of the following questions is "yes," you need to make changes to the index entries.

- ❑ Does a main entry for the name of the product have numerous subentries? (It shouldn't.)
- ❑ Do insignificant differences in capitalization or plurals cause separate index entries to appear, rather than one entry with more than one subentry?
- ❑ Do duplicate main entries occur, with no indication of the difference between them?
- ❑ Do some entries have too much detail? For example, a main entry may have several subentries, but all the subentries point to the same topic.
- ❑ Do any "see" references point to an entry that does not have subentries?
- ❑ Are any concepts and synonyms missing from the index?
- ❑ Are any entries or subentries irrelevant?
- ❑ Do any main entries have only one subentry?

Reviewing the help system as a whole

Refer to Chapter 5, "Avoiding Common Problems," Chapter 7, "Providing Navigation and Context," and Chapter 8, "Meeting the Needs of Novices to Experts," for details.

- ❑ Have the specified topic types been provided? Have they been written in the specified style and do they contain the specified information?
- ❑ Are the topic types appropriate for the audience?
- ❑ If information types have been used in the project, has each topic been assigned to the appropriate information type?
- ❑ Has the writer enabled the various tools (Bookmarks, Favorites, History list) that readers might use? Would they be helpful?
- ❑ Can users control where and when the help is displayed?
- ❑ Can users choose what help features they want to see?

Visual aids

If visual aids are used in the help file:

- ❑ Are they helpful or are they confusing or irrelevant?
- ❑ Are navigational icons or colors used consistently? That is, do similar topics have the same icons, used in the same way, placed in the same spot in each topic?
- ❑ Is the meaning of the icons clear to the reader, or is some quick and easy way provided for the reader to find out what the icon means?

Integrated systems

- ❑ Do the links lead users to relevant information?
- ❑ Do links to the Web make it clear that's where they go?
- ❑ Is vital information installed on the user's system?
- ❑ Can PDF files or other relevant documents be opened outside the application?

If the answer to either of the following questions is "yes," you need to make appropriate changes.

- ❑ Should some information be moved from other files to the help system?
- ❑ Should some information be moved from the help system to other files?

Browse sequences

If the help file has browse sequences, check every sequence.

- ❑ What is the purpose of this browse sequence?
- ❑ Is the order of topics in the sequence logical?
- ❑ If any topics have internal links to other topics, can readers get back to the sequence if they follow one of those links?

If the answer to any of the following questions is "yes," you need to make appropriate changes.

- ❏ Are irrelevant topics included?
- ❏ Are any topics missing that should be in the sequence?
- ❏ Should linked topics be part of the sequence?

Reviewing embedded help

Refer to Chapter 8, "Meeting the Needs of Novices to Experts." In addition to the usual issues of terminology, consistency, and so on, consider these issues:

- ❏ Can users turn off the embedded help if they don't want it or find it annoying? If so, can they easily get help when they do want it?
- ❏ Is the information in tooltips, mouseovers, or messages relevant? Does it make sense in context? (Short phrases may be too cryptic.)

Reviewing the contents of help topics

Refer to Chapter 3, "Developing Specifications," and Appendix A, "Sample Plans and Specifications," for details.

- ❏ Does the topic contain all the information the reader needs at that point? If not, does it include links to other topics that fill in the gaps?
- ❏ Can you tell how this topic fits in with what you want to do?
- ❏ If a topic tells you how to do something, do you know where to find that function in the application?
- ❏ Does the topic tell you what you need to do first, before you do this step?
- ❏ Does each topic include the cross-references required by the specifications?
- ❏ Are text links self-explanatory? Do readers get a good idea of what they will find if they click on the link?

If the answer to either of the following questions is "yes," you need to make appropriate changes.

- ❏ Do cross-reference links within the text distract the reader?
- ❏ Do text links lead to unnecessary glossary and other small pop-up windows?

Show-me topics

❑ Are the links to these topics presented in the same way?

❑ Are all the show-me topics of the same type (either animated or static) or does it matter?

❑ Have the show-me topics been written in the style specified in the design, and do they contain the specified information?

❑ Does the help give unambiguous context for the item, so the user can find it on the interface?

❑ If a control is not available or not visible under some conditions, does the help say so?

Coaches

❑ Does each coach have enough explanation to assist novice users?

❑ Have the coaches been written in the style specified in the design, and do they contain the specified information?

❑ Does the help give unambiguous context for the item, so the user can find it on the interface?

❑ If a control is not available or not visible under some conditions, does the help say so?

Tutorials

❑ Do tutorials give a clear indication of how long they might take to run, what the user will learn, how to run them, how to quit, and whether users can return to the place where they stopped?

❑ Are the controls unambiguous and located in the same place on each page?

❑ Are users told clearly that anything they do in the tutorial will not affect real data?

Wizards

❑ Does the wizard have enough explanation on each page to assist novice users in making a decision?

❑ If not, can users get more information without closing the wizard?

❑ Have the wizards been written in the style specified in the design, and do they contain the specified information?

Copyediting

Refer to Chapter 10, "Copyediting and Production Editing," for details.

- ❑ Prepare and regularly add to the project style guide.
    - ❑ Primary source materials (dictionary, other style guide, design guide)
    - ❑ Version of English to use, and any variations
    - ❑ System of measurement to use, and any variations
    - ❑ Capitalization style for headings, vertical lists, and figure and table captions
    - ❑ Punctuation for running lists, vertical lists, and other situations
    - ❑ Required document elements
    - ❑ Topic length and content
    - ❑ Cross-reference style
    - ❑ Requirements for captions to figures and tables, and text references to them
    - ❑ Highlighting use
    - ❑ Numbers: when to spell out or use numerals; the use of commas or spaces in numbers over 999
    - ❑ Word use (for example, company-specific, platform-specific, or product-specific terms; acronyms and abbreviations; and words to be avoided)
    - ❑ Use of limited English, if relevant
    - ❑ Caution, danger, and warning notices: wording and usage
    - ❑ Index style, and guidelines on wording of entries
    - ❑ Glossaries, bibliographies, and footnotes: what style, and when to use
    - ❑ Trademarks: how to indicate and acknowledge
    - ❑ Writing style
- ❑ Copyedit the online help, looking for most of the same problems that you would check in printed documents; for example:
    - ❑ Spelling mistakes and misused words
    - ❑ Jargon, unfamiliar words, and inconsistent use of terms
    - ❑ Incorrect grammar or punctuation
    - ❑ Topic titles unclear, misleading, too long, or not in approved style
    - ❑ Long, wordy sentences or paragraphs that should be turned into lists
    - ❑ Misused or inconsistently used bulleted or numbered lists
    - ❑ List items not in parallel style
    - ❑ Inconsistent capitalization and punctuation
    - ❑ Inconsistent use of bold, italics, color, or other highlighting

- ❑ Inconsistent style and presentation of procedures
- ❑ Long, complex, or branching procedures, or too many sub-procedures
- ❑ Steps out of order in procedures
- ❑ Link text unclear, misleading, too long, too short, or not in approved style
- ❑ Too many links, or links too close together
- ❑ Any other deviations from specifications

Production editing

Refer to Chapter 10, "Copyediting and Production Editing," for details.

- ❑ Have all the errors from the copyedit been corrected?
- ❑ Are all necessary topics in the final build of the help file?
- ❑ Have all topics that should *not* be in the final build been removed from the help file?
- ❑ Have all notes from one team member to another been removed from the final help file?
- ❑ Are any graphics blurry, the wrong size, or unnecessary?
- ❑ Do any hotspots (links) have these problems?
    - ❑ Poor choice of words
    - ❑ Too close together in text or image maps
    - ❑ Too large or too small
    - ❑ Not easy to distinguish from other text
    - ❑ Too many colors
- ❑ Do any tables display incorrectly?
- ❑ Are any tables too wide or too long?
- ❑ Do any bulleted and numbered lists display incorrectly?
- ❑ Is indentation too much or inconsistent?
- ❑ Are help window sizes and placement inconsistent?

Usability testing

Refer to Chapter 11, "Usability Testing on a Budget," for details.

- ❑ Define testing objectives and methods.
    - ❑ Goals for the test
    - ❑ Audience
    - ❑ What to measure
    - ❑ Data collection methods

❑ Develop usability test plan.

    ❑ What to test when

    ❑ Who to do the testing

❑ Write test materials (scenarios for testers to follow).

❑ Recruit participants.

❑ Set up test environment.

❑ Conduct the test.

❑ Analyze and report on the results.

❑ Prioritize problems and required changes.

Updates and corrections to this chapter can be found on Hentzenwerke's Web site, **www.hentzenwerke.com**. Click "Catalog" and navigate to the page for this book.

Index

Note that you can download the PDF file for this book from **www.hentzenwerke.com** (see the section "How to Download the Files" at the beginning of this book). The PDF is completely searchable and will provide additional keyword lookup capabilities not practical in an index.